GRACE UNDER PRESSURE

One Congregation's Testimony

F. DEAN LUEKING

SKIPWORTH PRESS, INC.
RICHMOND, VIRGINIA 23227

For further information: Skipworth Press, Inc.
P.O. Box 9367, Richmond, VA 23227

Library of Congress No. 79-65568
ISBN—0-931804-03-5

Contents

Other Books by F. Dean Lueking

Mission in the Making
Grace Under Pressure
A Century of Caring
While It is Day
Grace Under Pressure (II)

To the Grace People
with respect and affection

Foreword

The author of *Grace Under Pressure* says that at least twice I dropped in fortuitously at crisis moments in his ministry to his congregation. This time I am dropping by at his invitation to say a few opening words about him and his congregation in a time of conflict.

I make no pretense to objectivity. In my hierarchy of Christian gifts the experience of friendship has to rank near the top, and in the annals of friendship my family and I could have hoped for nothing better in this brief life than to be webbed in with the Luekings. As one sample: Pastor Lueking is baptismal sponsor or godfather to our oldest son who, in turn, is godfather to the youngest Lueking, his namesake Joel. If that suggests a sort of intimacy or spiritual incest, fine; let it symbolize a kinship we treasure.

Despite the evident bias, I hope also to be fair-minded enough as a long-time observer of American religion to say that the struggles of Grace Lutheran Church deserve to be rehearsed far beyond the confines of Lutheranism. They help make up a case study of conflict in social institutions as well as of witness to the Christian Gospel in a time of testing.

The literature on social conflict is impressively large but usually abstract and impersonal. The shelf of books about the life of parishes is largely restricted to anniversary histories, too many of which gloss over the struggles in order merely to chronicle the high points or to make everything appear in the best light. A third category of books are reveries by emeriti, a pleasant genre of reminiscence but still a form of expression which tends to gloss over the agonies which Christians under trial have to face. And there are "how to" books, which trade on the successes of successful parishes.

"Grace" has so many things going for it, many of them capable of being glimpsed on these pages, that any number of "how to" volumes could issue forth and maybe in a more serene time many will. But in a time when Christians are seeking redirection, when they are trying to learn how to fuse their commitment to Christ and truth with a need to be civil and concordant with each other, it is good to have an almost microscopic study of a disturbed cell struggling for regained health.

I have put the matter in entirely too dramatic terms. One could be a participant on many levels in congregational life in this Illinois parish and hardly be aware of any problems. Our family attends several times a year, usually for monthly Bach cantatas or Christmas at midnight or Easter at dawn. To hear "the divine elemental roar of the organ"—a phrase I first heard from a former organist at Grace—fighting trumpets and oboes all undergirded by tympani whomped by a manufacturer of drums is to be placed near what Paul Tillich calls "a revelatory constellation." Then comes a silence for talking alone with God, and singing of a kind that stirs depths we thought we had lost.

Martin Luther said that the church was a "Mundhaus," a mouth house, that the Word of God is not so much to be *geschrieben* as *geschrieen*. But the pastors at Grace do not have to shout. The sacrament of sound waves occurs there so frequently that when the baptized saints (and their dropping-by friends and fellow-worshippers) gather in front of the pulpit, they are ready to hear very down-to-earth applications of the saving Word to their lives. Oft have my sons sat there, their stopwatches set as sons' stopwatches tend to be, and just as they grew restless at the eighteen minute point "Uncle Dean" has zinged them with some first-person account of how the Word has lived in the experience of some member that week.

The education of children, the singing of great choirs,

support of controversial causes, adult learning experiences, engagement with the needs of local and larger community, evangelization—all these go on with impressive regularity. Too bad, is it not, that they cannot be the focus of this book in our mean and demoralized times.

Or could it be that they do go on on a scale proportionate to the size and power of that congregation precisely because it was long preparing to be tested, faced the test, and now is outlasting it? And is it not also the case that vitality elsewhere is born of such tests, as readily in tiny and by-the-way congregations as in visible powerhouses in Chicago suburbs? I recall a predecessor of the author regularly pointing to apathetic parishes around the community and remarking on their unused potential "because they had never been tested and had never met their test."

The demonic has not departed from the world. The occultation of dark forces still threatens the church. One can almost hear the flapping of wings from nether regions in the voices of hate directed against the clarity and purity of the Gospel. Some times we may envy the minister and people who are granted the freedom to spend their whole careers exempt from confrontation with such forces, secure in their serenity. But maybe more to be envied are those who have grown from their position in the front line, who were minding their own business but were called to heroism. On a cosmic scale we have seen this in the churches under Nazism or Communism. On a more petite scale, but never an insignificant one to those engaged with it, can be the testing that can come from the apparent children of light, nice people who find other Christians *de trop,* unable to occupy the same terrain, not fit for life in the Church of God.

When such forces closed in on Grace Church, the pastors were by no means alone. Generations of well-prepared lay people made all the difference. But I have observed frequently that the strength of the laity has difficulty emerging where pastoral leadership is weak. So I must return for a last time to a paragraph or two about the author, who was never solitary but always focal. How well equipped and poised was Dean Lueking for the tasks before him.[2]

The answer: terribly.

Let this embarrass him, since he knows I will protest if he censors it out. Back in seminary a classmate who wearied of watching Lueking remain patient when the temper of others gave out once shouted, "The problem with you, Dean, is that you were born without Original Sin. You'll never understand the rest of us!" For a lay translation of the seminary world I must say that this classmate was given to high hyperbole, and that the temptations that come to the apparently innocent are most beguiling. In this case, the patient one seemed invulnerable to the temptations to be cruel and hateful. Who could know what was in the depth of his heart?

Yet through these pastoral years, Lueking still has made the mistake of expecting the best of people, of underestimating cunning and vileness. Through the years of crisis the Martys and the Luekings have shared monthly Thursdays at the Chicago Symphony Orchestra concerts, our evenings of "secular transcendence." We precede these with dinner at the Cliff Dwellers Club atop orchestra hall. How he and we needed such stolen hours of retreat! Yet each month he would arrive from parking the car brimming with good will and—where did he draw the resources?—residual zest. Yes, everything is going well. Yes, everything will turn out fine. Yes, the Gospel will win out. Finally it would be up to his spouse to snort a pleasant rejoinder to the effect that the forces arrayed against him were not taking the evening off. But she, too, would instantly capitulate. A rule: never to let things like this topic cloud a moment of sabbath, siesta, or fiesta. I am amazed as I read these pages to learn how constant and consistent was the struggle during all these years, so rarely did we talk about it.

Were the stakes high enough to merit such resistance to a coup in the church body to which Grace was related? Certainly a couple of thousand parishes whose evangelical outlook matches that of Grace and its pastors have settled down for quiet attrition and subvert service back in that church body. I know many forty-year-old men who figure that they can somehow endure their ministry back in the security of the old corral, knowing there is something still to feed on and there is feeding to do even there. It is not my business to judge them. I also know others who have rationalized existence there when they found no other option. Their people have an evangelical spirit, some things can be accomplished for part of another generation, there is too much lethargy in the people to merit stirring them up to make a move into exile, so why not put the best face on things? And that, too, is something a Dean Lueking might regret but would never judge. He and his people could only say that when the test came to them, they had to join with hundreds of other congregations in resistance.

To people only an eighth of an inch away from their former church body, it would be difficult to see what the fuss was about. Emphatically Grace congregation remains in congruence with its position when in 1929 it bought the land on which it erected a church building. That is, it teaches and preaches the scripture "in accordance with the rules, regulations and customs" set forth in the Confession of its former church body, accepting without reservation the Scriptures "as the written Word of God and the only rule and norm of faith and of practice" and the ecumenical creeds and the Lutheran confessional writings "as . . . true and unadulterated statement and exposition of the Word of God."

But between 1929 and 1979 something happened to the host body. In the eyes of Grace, it fell under the spirit of what Paul Tillich called *heteronomy,* appeal to authority other than the Word of God. Most definitely and unconstitutionally, it "decided . . . matters of doctrine and of conscience" by majority vote, and not the Word of God. Truth came to be reckoned as that which 51% of the elected delegates to each year's convention called true. The heart of the Lutheran Reformation and the Pauline Gospel was at stake when, in effect, Luther's old position that "councils can err" was overturned or the Pauline position that Christian congregations should not be back under the Law was reversed.

Accompanying this heteronomous move was another one, the ostensible doctrinal issue of the struggle. One can participate in the preaching and teaching at Grace Church for years and never hear wavering in assent to the full scriptural truth as Lutherans confess it. In the words of a conservative Lutheran who wrote before the synodical battle of 1969 broke out, Grace Church believed that "the believer does not accept the absolute authority of the Scriptures as *a prior* truth, but because he has learned to know Christ as his divine Savior . . . (F. E. Mayer, *The Religious Bodies of America*. St. Louis: Concordia, 1954 p. 140). But now the people who did come with *a priori* views of scriptural inerrancy made their philosophies official by majority vote. To Grace this was "teaching for doctrines the commandments of men," the highest kind of idolatry and arrogation to the self of an authority God granted to no humans. Give a faction or a leadership the power to set up that principle and then decide annually what that inerrant scripture teaches and they can do anything. Literally anything. And they began to do so.

So Grace joined the resistance. Its participation was not more elegant, eloquent, poignant, or courageous than was that of hundred of other parishes. It was more visible because of the congregation's prominence, its location on the edge of a denominational college, and the national recognition of its pastor, who was also for a couple of years visible in the inter-congregational attempts to hold back the night.

The author's relative innocence and naïvete, his inability to learn how to gird for political battle, provides some of the unwitting humor of this book. Because the congregation functioned so effectively on so many levels, it did not nurture a hassling assembly of the whole; its congregation-wide meetings were the only elements of Grace that could be characterized as harboring "creative apathy." So one night the right-wing minority in the congregation amassed forces (14 votes among 1800 members) and thus out voted the more representative group, thereby nominating for president of the synod the leader of the right-wing coup instead of a moderate candidate supported nationally by the pastor. That night I have no doubt Pastor Lueking found himself capable of drawing at last on his reserves of Original Sin to feel a bit spiteful.

Let me also correct one other impression that these pages may leave. When the vote to move on was taken, 199 people were not ready to go. This may seem that almost 200 members, one-ninth of the whole, agreed with the position of their former church body. While Lueking leaves clues and traces to the effect that this was not true, it should be said explicitly many of these votes did not agree with the "heteronomous" and "a prioristic" positions of the new leadership of their church body, though thank God they would not have used those terms. They were nostalgic or timid, webbed and bonded to families that did not comprehend the struggle, or hopeful people who thought against hope and reason that their witness within might make a difference. The hard-core support of the synodical position belonged to about four dozen people.

When all was said and done, was the battle worth it? For its victory, Grace did not get peace. The hard-core people and the old synod engaged in rear-guard actions that retard or complicate the witness and service of the congregation several seasons later. Grace did not become part of a new majority in its church body, and was not even free (by the terms of a 1929 land purchase agreement) to link up with another church body at all—except in spirit. This it did, with all the rest of Lutheranism, 70,000,000 strong, a cohort denied congregational fellowship back in the old confines, and with millions of other Christians with which it moved into deeper fellowship. But the world is not reformed, nor is the church.

I believe the importance of this action, as it is important in every congregation of every church body, lies in what I call *intrinsicality*. There are moments in life when one must do what one must do because it is the nature of integrity to demand that it be done. No one need hear about it, no one dare calculate the merit of the action, no one could assess possible valuable outcomes.

Jews in concentration camps witnessed to what was in them not because to do so would give them external freedom or victory or would assure them an extra day's physical existence. They did what they had to do because something deep in their nature would have been denied had they allowed the evil to have its way in silence. The Christian martyrs to Nazism finally spoke up not because then we could tell their story. We do not even know the names of most of them, and have no way of knowing how many witnessed. But they lived and died and live because they were firm in a sense of truth and grace that called them to the intrinsic value of testimony.

It is a long way from Germany in the forties to the relative quiet of American church life three decades and more later, and it would be bizarre to confuse the scale. But there are Presbyterians, Episcopalians, Roman Catholics, Methodists, and people of many other Christian stripes, who in the quiet of their lives find or will find that gradually or suddenly—who knows when or how?—the basic test of their life together can come. I would like to think that this little book is one more set of verses in the modern Acts of the Apostles, one among many examples of steadfastness and courage and, ultimately, of joy, that will show how the Holy Spirit has not withdrawn his Presence from the world of Original Sinners, in which the New Creation has begun to leave its mark and sign.

Martin E. Marty
Chicago, Ill.

April, 1979

CHAPTER 1

A Congregation Decides

It was an evening to remember.

None of us present in the sanctuary of Grace Church that Indian summer evening will ever forget it.

The stately Gothic sanctuary was filled to the doors, and some latecomers were standing in the narthex as the 8 o'clock hour approached on September 20, 1977. The people of this congregation had come home from their work locations in all parts of Chicago and had their suppers taken care of in good time. A dozen or so college students had managed to get rides back to River Forest—some from distances of several hundred miles. They cared enough to be present. Interested friends of the congregation, many of whom had followed with keen interest the course of the congregation's struggle with key issues of faith and church life over the past four or five years, took their places in the balconies. I noticed those in the front row were leaning forward with their elbows on the oak railing, and their eyes upon the members occupying the pews below.

Some 650 voting members of Grace came to church on that third Tuesday evening of the month, and several hundred more non-voting parishioners and friends of the congregation brought the number to over 800.

They came to decide whether to remain in or withdraw from the denomination which had been our organizational home for over 75 years. Most of us present had been in congregations affiliated with the Lutheran Church-Missouri Synod since our earliest days, and our loyalties, associations, friendships have been influenced deeply by these denominational ties. The air was charged with strongly felt convictions, pro and con. I sensed it even before walking into the sanctuary ten minutes or so before the meeting was to begin.

My intention had been to get home for a quick supper with the family and return with Beverly and our older children for the meeting, but I discovered what everybody knows about his appetite when something of critical, long-range importance is at hand. It just isn't there! And so I spent the hours preceeding 8 p.m. hunched over my typewriter in my study, working and re-working the brief pastoral message I wanted to bring these people I love very much. It is hardly usual for me to write out a speech for my fellow Christians of Grace who come for a church meeting—but this was hardly a casual occasion. My train of thought and concentration were interrupted by the phone ringing, mostly people who wanted to make sure they had the time and date right for the meeting they did not want to miss. One visitor stopped in around six. The minute I saw him at the door I not only felt glad but immediately asked him to give me a quick critique of the message I wanted our people to hear from me. Martin Marty is a friend who somehow senses just the right time to stop by with support, encouragement, and a well-placed reminder that Christ is alive and well in His church and world and we can therefore depend upon Him to make His presence felt and His peace known when the adrenalin runs faster than normal. I remembered another well-timed, brief drop-in by Marty when the time was especially right. It was fifteen years earlier, the funeral day of Otto Geiseman, whose death brought to a conclusion a magnificent forty year pastorate in Grace Church. An hour or so before that Service, when I was again entrenched before the typewriter getting my thoughts and words in as good order as possible under the circumstances, Marty stopped in just long enough to speak a half dozen sentences of brotherly encouragement before I conducted the Memorial Service for a pastor under whom we had both served as fledgling assistants.

Another visitor knocked on the door at half past seven. Marvin Dumler, all six feet four of him, makes an imposing and always welcome sight in my study. He is a seasoned man of the faith, who has the gift of an uncommon measure of sound judgment, even temper, and level disposition which he gained from his earliest days on a Kansas farm. He was to serve as chairman of the meeting that evening, and we could not be better served. Earlier in the afternoon he had come by from his office at Concordia Teachers College to review with me in point-by-point fashion the correct parliamentary procedures for the evening. It was not an easy assignment for this excellent, unflappable man, to serve as chairman once again as he had done so often before. As a professional teacher in the church and a faculty member of Concordia, Marvin knew that the outcome of the evening would have a far-reaching personal impact upon him and his family and other teaching colleagues who were employees of the Missouri Synod as well as members of Grace Church. But whatever anxieties there were inside of him did not rob him of his down-to-earth manner and his sense of humor. When I mentioned to him that I had a "little speech" to make to the members before the debate began and the voting took place, he inquired whether the "little speech" was sermon length ala Sunday morning or considerably shorter. We both grinned and both agreed that this was no evening for the pastor to filibuster. The message from me was under five minutes and as any parishioner from Grace can readily testify, that is well below par when contrasted with Sunday morning preaching time!

One more time Marvin and I went over the format for the evening. All was in order.

I walked into the sanctuary from the side entrance, past the baptismal font and on to the center aisle of the nave.

It was faces my eyes were seeking. I wanted to *see* something of the hopes and fears, the misgivings and the anticipation of the men and women of Grace whom I have been privileged and know and to serve for nearly a quarter of a century.

And so, down the center aisle I went—row by row. The church was filled with sounds of people buzzing in conversation and greeting. Most of them, that is. Some sat quietly, receiving my brief greeting with a smile and warm handshake. But they did not want to take much time for greetings and chatter, nor should they. Their senses of soul told them that the congregation was at a milestone and turning point. After tonight it would never be the same. I respect that sense of seriousness; it was altogether appropriate for the occasion.

Some of the members did not turn their faces my way as I came along. A few faces were set in a stony, almost seething mood of anger. These were members who were upset and confused as to why the whole question of withdrawing from a denomination ever arose in the first place. Such people need a focus for their anger. They need to be able to locate their frustration in somebody, and that somebody was me. The presence of so many parishioners in the church that night bothered them, it gave them a sinking feeling that their hopes of staying in a denomination they felt so much a part of were threatened. They could not help but see in me the symbol of a pastoral leadership they opposed, on this particular issue at least.

Those deeply unhappy, worried faces taught me something.

How short our memories are! One of the women who could not bring herself to look me in the eye or accept my hand extended in greeting had nearly died from burns suffered in a flash fire in her kitchen a half dozen years ago. In repeated pastoral visits to the intensive care unit of the hospital in which she endured a long, painful, but successful recovery, she had never turned her face to the wall in refusal of the Word of Him I came to represent. She always welcomed me, even if only with her eyes because it was too much for her to speak. But now it was different. The thought of her congregation no longer a part of the Missouri Synod was enough, at that moment, to make her lose her manners. She did utter one short sentence as she stared straight ahead: "I wish I had died instead of living to see this meeting." Her sister seated beside her told her not to say such things. But perhaps she had to say it and I had to hear it. It was a revealing thought she expressed, and there were others around the room who would say something similar—though not in those words perhaps. What it revealed was the thing the late Paul Tillich described with such penetrating insight. When our religious sensibilities are pressed beyond the ordinary it becomes clearer as to where our real security lies. *Aut*onomy signifies our placement of ultimate dependence in the self. *Hetero*nomy places that full thrust of the heart in some other thing (such as a church body). *Theo*nomy puts the heart of our being at rest in the living God.

To be sure, the agenda of the evening was not phrased in words which asked us where our ultimate trust was anchored, in God or in a denomination. And parishioners have a perfect right to feel glum, irked, and strongly opposed to a decision which would rearrange an organizational relationship of three-quarters of a century duration. Further, those who could not find it within themselves to offer a cheery smile and a friendly handshake must not be scorned.

But the underlying issue as defined by Tillich was really the issue and remains so for us all. Who comes first? We are taught by Christ Himself to love God with our whole heart and strength and mind. *Theonomy* is the goal toward which His Spirit leads us. But along the way there are obstacles to that goal, including the obstacle of putting loyalty to a denomination over loyalty to God.

But the other side of that coin is the disregard of the truth that to belong to Christ is to belong to His people. A denomination is, after all, people. It is the particular place in which something of the universality of Christ's church universal is experienced. To withdraw from it or to change a relationship to it cannot be a matter of caprice or self-centeredness.

And so every mood in the faces of the people of Grace had meaning, and it was not as though there was just one way for the emotions of the members to be judged. Those few minutes before the meeting were an opportunity for me to grow in the awareness that a congregation is always a gathering of people at different points of conviction, preference, needs, and hopes. What good is that if one salutes only those who think his way?

The meeting began.

The prayers were offered.

The first thing for the assembly to determine was the length of time for each person to speak. The chairman asked the people to respond to some suggestions. Six minutes per person? Or five or four? After all, the idea was not to cut people off if they had something they really needed time to say. To be sure, the previous *three years* had given members repeated opportunities to say what they wanted to say. But this was an evening to determine a direction of uncommon importance. What was the will of the majority?

"Two minutes!" someone from the assembly proposed, and before two minutes passed the seconding motion was made, the vote taken, and the matter was passed. Such a severe restriction on time for each speaker to express his or her views struck me as unfortunate. I had agreed earlier with a senior member of Grace, Wilfred Kruse, one whose granite-like sense of fairness to all points of view qualified him as a much respected elder statesman of the congregation, who had stated his willingness to stay in session all night long if that was what was required for all to have their say. But the two minute time margin, passed resoundingly, indicated that the assembly wanted speakers to get to the point promptly since most had made up their minds on the matter before coming to the meeting.

Dr. Dumler proposed that those who wished to speak take their places in the front rows, those supporting the recommendations to withdraw from the Synod on one side and those opposing it on the other. Pro and con speakers were to alternate; the front pews on either side quickly filled up.

Then the motion of the Church Council was read:

> "After several years of study and discussion of issues related to the controversey in the Lutheran Church-Missouri Synod and its effect upon our congregation, the Church Council makes the following recommendation to the Voter's Assembly:
>
> THAT GRACE EVANGELICAL LUTHERAN CHURCH, RIVER FOREST, ILLINOIS, WITHDRAW ITS MEMBERSHIP FROM THE LCMS EFFECTIVE OCTOBER 1, 1977 AND CONTINUE ITS CHRISTIAN MISSION AND MINISTRY AS AN INDEPENDENT LUTHERAN CONGREGATION ACCORDING TO THE STANDARDS OF FAITH SET FORTH IN ARTICLE II OF THE CONSTITUTION OF THE CONGREGATION."

The recommendation had been mailed to each member of the congregation several weeks earlier. It carried the signatures of the entire membership of the Church Council (19 men and women) plus four pages of explanatory information supporting the proposal plus a two page legal opinion from the firm of Kirkland and Ellis stating their opinion that a move to independent status would not give the Synod the right to purchase the property and buildings of Grace Church according to a 1929 contract—about which, more later.

The entire packet of information had been worked on carefully by the Church Council. It was an effort to set forth clearly the direction the congregation was asked to take and the reasons for it. It never occurred to me that anyone would take exception to its printed format. But—several months later—I talked with a member whose active part in the congregation for several years had been a lift for us all and who had been supportive of the evangelical spirit of Grace all along. But this mailing had come across to her as unfair and one-sided. Where was the other side's viewpoint? Her question puzzled me. For months we had heard pros and cons and heard all sides of the question. A continuing difficulty through the preceeding years had been to find advocates of "the other side". What existed, of course, were other sides. People opposed the idea of leaving the denomination for varied reasons, and had said so in letters and other communications circulated in the congregation for three years previous. All this notwithstanding, we could have done things better in preparing the materials for the members to study. While others had given us encouragement and appreciation for the document that was mailed out previous to the voter's assembly, I will not forget the straightforward criticism of a thoughtful woman. She did more than offer her criticism. She is no longer with us in the fellowship of the congregation.

One by one the speakers stepped quickly to the microphone placed at the head of the pews, and each was conscious of the difficulty of getting his or her points across in two minutes. A timekeeper was posted at the side of the podium, with a buzzer reminding each that so many seconds were left before two minutes had elapsed.

I was interested in the group of fellow members who took their places on the "against" side. The most strident, accusatory, and vociferous opposers of the congregation's direction in general and my ministry in particular did not come forward to speak. Their absence from the speakers' row was not accidental. Some strategy planning had apparently occurred beforehand, and there was prudence in the decision as to who would and would not speak.

First up was Henry Eichelberg, a man who holds his convictions firmly and expresses himself in plain words which come from his heart. He advocated staying with the Synod, because he felt that the direction of the present Synodical administration was right and necessary. In his judgment Grace Church had been led down the primrose path, as he put it, by Pastor Lueking. There had not been adequate attention to the doctrinal issues which underlay the whole controversy, he added, and no good cause could be served by pulling out. Plain-spoken, to the point, from the heart: Henry did not offend me personally with his words. I sensed a ripple of negative emotion from the assembly when he characterized my pastoral leadership as journey down the primrose path, but I know Henry better than many. It was not an effort to be personally vindictive. It was just the way he saw it, and that was his way of saying what he saw. I recalled the time he told me how it happened that he came to Grace Church. He had grown up in a home without active church life. His neighbor across the street, Fred Gahl, was also the mailman. Fred's unpretentious ways of quietly living the Christ-like life impressed Henry (as well as myself and many more). And thus a channel of the Spirit was opened up to this man who had since moved up to a position of leadership in his business as a manufacturer of a remarkable device for detecting and photographing objects in near darkness. Some years ago I had called Henry and asked him if I might spend a little time with him at his place of work, to give me a better insight into those things which occupied his mind and energies between Sundays. It was a good visit, mutually enjoyable and beneficial. In more recent times, however, Henry had become more and more a part of the opposition group in the congregation. I regretted the subtle distancing that was occurring, yet always found Henry ready to say exactly what he was thinking. That is a quality to be respected, even when what one is thinking is the polar opposite of my own viewpoint.

Next came the first speaker supporting the withdrawal motion. Walter Christopher has been a part of Grace Church for over fifty years. He has served in nearly every elected office of the parish, and is one of those faithful men who make the ministry truly satisfying. Walter is an attorney, and accustomed to getting straight to the heart of the matter. Grace Church, he said, has always tried to live with the love of Christ and the spirit of the Gospel uppermost. The past half dozen years have brought increasing confrontation with a new administration and new directions in the Synod at large. In advocating withdraw he was, in fact, urging us to stay in the mainstream of Lutheranism and Christendom. Our spirit was not compatible with sectarianism; we did not wish to change the character of our spiritual direction. His appeal was for continuity with our past, rather than in-increasing conflict with a Synod which had changed from the denomination we had all known and loved. Two minutes came too soon. The cutoff buzzer stopped Walter in the midst of a sentence. At least, I noted to myself mentally, each speaker should be able to finish the sentence in which the time limit was reached!

Then came Elfrieda Miller, a member of Grace for over a half century and a teacher of many of our children in her years of faithful service as a faculty member of Grace School. As always, her thoughts were expressed in well-chosen words and offered in a kindly spirit of sincere appeal. In her mind, moving out of the denomination was wrong. Too many historical ties would be broken, too much difficulty would result in our relations with nearby Concordia College. And what about a meaningful mission program at home and abroad? Independence, as Miss Miller saw it, was opening the door to self-serving and a turning inward by the congregation that could not bring blessing. Elfrieda did not claim that the Synod was flawless, but she did speak from her heart when she stated that the strong doctrinal cohesion of the Missouri Synod would be tragic to separate from. While she respected and loved fellow parishioners who differed from her, she begged us not to leave the denomination that has been home for so many decades. Her words were effectively spoken.

Then came Paul Bouman, all six feet four of him uncomfortably scrunched down so that his voice could be picked up by the microphone attached to the speaker's stand. No individual among us is held in higher esteem than this man who is organist, music director, and upper grade teacher in Grace School. His father had been a Missouri Synod pastor in Minnesota. His wife's grandfather was president of the Missouri Synod during the post World War I years. Paul had been trained in Missouri Synod schools from kindergarten on, and had completed his full academy and college years at Concordia College with whom Grace shares the same square block in River Forest. He has taught in Missouri Synod schools and served as organist and choir director in the heartland of the Synod all his professional life. His past 25 years at Grace have been a time of unparalleled excellence in the ministry of music. The podium at which he was enduring a two minute ordeal was more familiar to him than any of us. From that podium he had directed choir concerts, Bach Cantatas, orchestral and instrumental ensembles, Advent concerts, Christman Eve concerts, and special Services of such rich musical heritage. He is a master with a baton in his hand, but to give a speech is a painful experience for him. I did not know he would speak. I had no knowledge of any of the speakers, pro or con. But there comes a time in person's life when all that he has seen with his own eyes and felt so deeply in his heart must be spoken. Mr. Bouman had written out perhaps a four or five minute speech, but he was determined to get it into the two minute space—regardless! And so he took us all—*presto*—through an impassioned testament from his heart concerning the incredibly harsh treatment given faithful Synodical missionaries, staff people, and Seminary faculty members (including his own brother, who had been one of the 45 members of Concordia Seminary faculty in St. Louis, Mo., who had chosen the way of exile rather than capitulate to the actions of Synodical President Jacob Preus nearly three years before). When Paul Bouman plays the organ, the congregation listens and follows. And now as Paul Bouman spoke, the result was not different among the majority of those present.

Among the other speakers speaking against were two that were noteworthy. One was a young man in his early twenties, who had compiled a splendid academic record at the University of Chicago and had chosen to go on to study for the pastoral ministry at Concordia Seminary in Ft. Wayne, Ind. Bill Kolb possesses courage as well as the strength of his convictions. He is an unusually serious-minded young man, whom I had come to know ten years ago in confirmation instruction. From time to time in his university years he would come by the study to talk of things on his mind. In his senior year at Chicago he had written a superb paper on an aspect of Augustine's thought related to contemporary ethical problems in American life. I was especially happy when he came in to speak of his interest in the ministerial vocation. Now he had spent one year at the seminary which had brought to him a strong influence of support for the current Synodical administration. Several months earlier Bill had heard me preach a sermon on the role of women in the church, which prompted him to write a letter to the district president suggesting that I should be investigated for possible false doctrine. The letter saddened me, not so much because of the proposal which got nowhere, but because of the rapidity with which a fine young man can be influenced in one year. His brief message to the congregation was for loyalty to the kind of Scriptural interpretation he was receiving at Ft. Wayne, an interpretive spirit which made him aware that he was at odds with his home parish and pastor.

Paul Grotelueschen's reasons for advocating staying in the Synod were markedly different from any of the previous speakers who opposed the Council motion. He wanted us to stay put so we could do everything possible within the Missouri Synod to offset the growing legalism and power politics that Grotelueschen had seen first hand as a faculty member at Concordia College and delegate to Synodical conventions. Paul Grotelueschen, like Paul Bouman, came from deep Missouri Synod roots. He personifies the genuine and remarkable loyalty to Christ and the Lutheran tradition which has stressed educating children in a school setting which is permeated by the Christian leaven. He is a winsome man, open-minded and with a heart brimming with Divine love. He and his wife have a family that is a mini-United Nations. Besides their own five children, they have taken into their household and raised to adulthood children from as far away as Hong Kong and as near as Chicago's black ghetto. Paul began his speech by looking straight at me, smiling from ear to ear, and telling the congregation that we can thank God for a ministry such as we have. He enumerated our blessings one after the other, and then made his point. Stay in and fight rather than switch! He was confident that a defeat of the motion to withdraw could not be misinterpreted as a repudiation of the Grace spirit. In fact he promised to make a motion supporting and affirming our ministry just as soon as the present motion could be defeated. I listened to that good hearted man with an enormous sense of gratitude for the privilege of being pastor to people of this spiritual caliber. Our disagreement over the particular motion at hand was penultimate. The ultimate truth about the life and purpose of the Christian congregation, that we serve by faith active through love, was truth in which Paul and I were completely one.

Among those supporting the motion two other speakers stood out in my mind.

Charlotte Scott is a newer member of Grace Church, but the quality of person who doesn't wait to be asked if there are ways in which her membership in the congregation can mean more than a name on the membership list. She is articulate, knowledgeable and utterly fearless in speaking her mind and heart before a church filled with people. Mrs. Scott came to Grace Church, she noted, because here she found a community of Christians who appeared willing to face facts in the denomination. She had done her homework before and after affiliating, and the whole sad range of Synodical actions over recent years which had intruded so directedly upon the lives and ministries of several hundred clergy and missionaries was known to her. She spoke strongly, asking her fellow parishioners to put aside fears and chart a course for the congregation which befits the Gospel spirit. She sharpened her message with the reminder that Grace congregation is a prize target for those who have taken over other segments of the Synod's life by the tactics of accusation, innuendo, and power politics. Withdrawal from the Synod, in her mind, was an act of needed witness to the Synodical leadership. It was the communicating of a message that a congregation will not be intimidated by a hierarchy that did not hesitate to label those who dissented from its tactics as "dissidents and rebels against the Word of God". No one yawned as Charlotte delivered the most impassioned speech of the evening.

But perhaps the most effective two minute address was that spoken by Jan Uitti, wife, mother, and teacher of the sixth grade in Grace School. Mrs. Uitti is the daughter of a Missouri Synod clergyman. She grew up in a parsonage, where the best of conservative Lutheranism surrounded her and conditioned her outlook. She married a clergyman of the Missouri Synod, who had followed his seminary graduation with pastoral experience and graduate study in Old Testament. Her upbringing puts her on the same level with all who advocate continuing in the Missouri Synod because of lifelong association with the Synod. Yet she spoke with a quiet firmness of the necessity now to step outside the denomination which had not only been her home all her life but also the graveyard for the careers of some of the most gifted pastors and teachers of the church. Her understated, restrained listing of the people who had been charged of false doctrine, harassed by Synodical authorities to the point of leaving their ministries or being dismissed from them struck a deep note of response. After all, the final measure of whether faith and hope and love are Christ-given or merely words is how people treat people. Janet let none of us forget the individuals and their families who have suffered one of the most grievous of all accusations, that of misleading others in matters of the faith. But in the space of two minutes she managed not only to cite the heart of the problem. She held before us the prospect of new directions, the continued faithfulness to Christ above all, the furtherance and enlargement of the evangelical spirit of love and openness as Lutheran Christians toward all to whom God leads us, the appreciation of gifted colleagues, not their ruination in constant accusation and purging. The words of Jan Uitti touched upon the heart of what everyone in the room sought, an end to the controversy which had been consuming the congregation increasingly in the past three years. Not all agreed with her proposal for finding liberation from it. But all could agree that this congregation could not continue its life and spiritual growth as inner dissension spreads its tentacles from month to month. Christians are to encounter the world and there expect the sparks to fly. But Christians are called to demonstrate to each other the acceptance by which Christ Himself has made us His sons and daughters through the forgiveness of our sins.

This profile of speakers underlines the truth that there is no single, simple way to draw the line between those who supported and opposed to withdrawal. The list of speakers is no cast of heroes and villains. No one, especially in the limits of several minutes, could hope to compress all the truth, wisdom, and sound judgement in one speech. The deeper issues underlying this spirited debate were not, could not, be fully revealed in the course of an evening. We all kept our mortality in mind, and spoke as people of Christ who see through a glass dimly.

After an hour and one half of speakers, there were no more members seated on the side of those opposing the motion. A speaker on the pro side called for the question, and the vote to close debate passed easily. Now came the time to vote.

Once again the chairman explained to the assembly that only those who were voting members of the congregation could vote. All others were asked to please take their place in the balcony as the ballots were distributed. Every detail of procedure for the entire meeting, including the wording of the ballot itself, had been gone over with scrupulous care by Dr. Marvin Dumler and myself beforehand. The thought had come to me that even the slightest, unintentional misstep in procedure might come back to haunt us later, a hunch which was appropriate in the light of events five months later.

Having listened so intently for nearly two hours, the assembly naturally needed to change the pace briefly. The hum of conversation which swept through the sanctuary was an understandable venting of the nervous energy built up through the course of the evening so far. Some needed to stand, stretch, smile, chat with people nearby. One gesture, however, struck me as absolutely unnecessary. The ballot boxes had been placed in the front of the church, one on either side. The member who quickly walked up to the ballot box on his side and lifted the cover to see if it was empty or perhaps stuffed with pre-marked ballots must have wondered if Grace congregation was an extension of Chicago's worst ward politics. On second thought, perhaps the gesture was not as gratuitous as it was indicative of a sense in a person who had been told so many half-truths and untruths about his congregation's pastor and leadership that he would have thought himself a hero to have shouted for everyone's attention with the damning evidence held aloft in his hand. The box, however, was empty. He sat down, saying nothing, even looking a little disappointed!

If the evening would have ended with the vote to close debate, I would have gone home grateful for the people whom I have been called by the Holy Spirit to serve. With feelings as taut as they were, and the consequences of the vote as sizeable as they turned out to be, the debate could have been a knock-down, dragout of a shouting match and full scale demonstration of the way Christians can hammer each other with hate. Grace congregation is comprised of people and pastor who have that capacity by reason of our fallen nature.

But it did not happen that way, nor has it ever happened that way in our midst. We have God to thank for the Spirit of forbearance and tolerant listening to one another across divided opinions. Just to be able to open up sensitive issues, simply to face them as honestly as possible, is a gift of no small value. Furthermore, the experience of venturing along the path of several years of regular and special meetings devoted to these demanding issues teaches people one of the prime gifts of the Spirit, that of being *for* another person in spite of being *against* what that person thinks.

Grace congregation had experienced a fine moment, quite apart from the vote and its outcome. I moved my folding chair up two steps from the sanctuary floor to the chancel level, so that I might be able to get a better look at these people of whom I was immensely proud and genuinely grateful.

There under the south balcony sat Marie Geiseman, widow of the former pastor and absolutely staunch in her support of those very principles which her husband had fostered over the forty years of his pastorate at Grace. Under the opposite balcony, sitting in her regular place where she can be found on Sunday mornings, was Augusta Cimaglio, 91 years, alert, amazingly spry, and determined to cast her vote for a Gospel-centered future for the congregation. Tight moments were nothing strange to her. She grew up on a South Dakota farm in a large German Lutheran family and knew how to shoot rattlesnakes in her front yard by age 14. As a young woman she had married an Italian immigrant and learned the demands of bridging the cultural gap between Dakota Lutherans and Napolitan Italians. Half way back on the pulpit side sat Florence Bruner together with her husband James. She came at the expense of much effort and pain to move from her home, where she carries on the daily battle against cancer. But Florence and Jim were there. Toward the back on the lectern side were a cluster of college students of the congregation who managed to get back home from their distant campuses and make their vote count. Joyce Hagen and Mark Bouman were back from Valparaiso University. Wendy Sievert had driven nonstop from Purdue in West Lafayette, Indiana, arriving just in time to take part in the meeting. Bill Kolb had come from Ft. Wayne and spoken his convictions. The sight of these people, and hundreds more who came forward to the ballot boxes, was one I shall not forget. Every mood and emotion was evident on their faces, happy, sad, and puzzled. But each is a person of Grace congregation. Each is God's own creation, and a member of Christ's People. That sight gladdened my heart. The saddening part of it, however, was the awareness that we would not all remain together as a congregation. That never happens anyway, in the course of events at Grace Church. In an average year, one hundred members will transfer because of business transfers to other parts of the country, retirement, traveling off to school, and death. But these are external causes for membership change. It is something else when membership change is due to internal reasons. A number of members had told me quietly in earlier weeks that if the vote to withdraw would pass, they would feel constrained to leave. Those who spoke of this necessity they felt did so without rancor. A number were faculty members in the Missouri Synod school system. They sensed that in some future time they would be told that they had to transfer to a congregation still affiliated with the Synod. Their preference was to make that decision themselves, before it would be made for them. Others expressed a strongly felt sense of moral obligation, that since they were drawing their paycheck from the Missouri Synod as employees in its system, they should belong to a member congregation. While I feel that continuance in the congregation by such splendid members is hardly an act lacking in moral integrity, I can understand the sense from which those convictions come. I respect them.

To collect some 650 votes in two boxes does not require a very long time. But to count them properly, and to re-check the count does.

Dr. Dumler and I had given forethought to the matter of counters, and had agreed upon four teams of two counters, each team being deliberately balanced with people of opposing views as far as we could surmise. I wondered if U.S. Presidential elections had tighter controls! The counters were chosen, and sent off to a nearby office room in the church.

There we all sat. No one made a move to leave. The chairman, assuming that pastors always have words to speak, asked me if I had any timely words to fill the space of time before the counters returned with the decision.

This was not time for me to speak.

It was a time for us all to sing.

Mr. Bouman took his place on turf more familiar to him, the organ bench on the south balcony. The church full of people became a church filled with the best of all the sounds I know—the congregation singing. And sing we did! "The Church's One Foundation", "Built On the Rock", "Jesus Christ Is Risen Today", "Lord, Keep Us Steadfast In Thy Word", "How Brightly Shines the Morning Star", "Praise To the Lord, the Almighty, the King of Creation", "Beautiful Savior", "Now Thank We All Our God", and "A Mighty Fortress Is Our God" were among the hymns the members sang with a fullness of heart and voice that matched the occasion which brought us together. I could not help but risk an occasional glance at some of the faces which had earlier in the evening been so glum. Such singing changed those faces! If not happy with humans that evening, they could not but show some spirit for God. The half hour or more of singing was worship at its best. We were at the brink of something new, unknown, and momentous. No one present could presume to know the outcome. Yet all could find wholeness, peace, and the encompassing presence of Christ in the songs of faith that brought us all together.

It did seem an uncommonly long time that the counters were out. But that was due to their extraordinary care in tallying the votes, then rechecking the count, coming to an unanimous decision that one ballot was disqualified (someone chose to editorialize on the whole evening instead of simply vote yes or no on the face of the ballot).

The tellers gave their report to Marvin Dumler through their chairman, Fred Spurgat.

Dr. Dumler asked for the attention of the assembly (as if that was difficult to achieve under the circumstances!).

He asked that the announcement of the vote be greeted with no applause, keeping in mind the feelings of people on all sides of the issue.

He then read the result: 425 for, 199 against. The motion passed. It had passed decisively. The step was taken.

The decision was accepted as the chairman had requested. A respectful quiet prevailed over the assembly as the hour had moved past 10:30 and people began to think about going home.

The senior elder, Dr. George Reinhardt, asked for the floor and moved the approval of the Church Council's arrangement for alternate retirement and medical coverage plans for the church staff, since the congregation would withdraw from the Synodical plans for retirement and medical coverage by withdrawing from the Synod. His motion was quickly passed without dissent.

Then the meeting was adjourned with pastoral prayer and the benediction.

Among the first people to reach me after the benediction was a reporter for CBS radio, asking for comment into a tape recorder/microphone when many other people were near at hand with whom I wanted to speak. I recall saying only the briefest, most general kinds of response to his questions and then reaching out for those whom I most wanted to speak.

I appreciated the calm, firm handshake of Dick Kirk, who with his wife, Marvel, expressed appreciation for the direction the evening had taken and enthusiasm for the future. Aline Kellerman was close by, with her husband Marvin. Her words of kindness and encouragement were consistent with her gracious spirit over the twenty four years I have known her. Morella Mensing was saddened by the decision, but wanted to say that the things which unite us in Christ are more lasting than the organizational structure of humans, which a Synod is. She is so right! Morella retired several years ago from her post at Grace School as first grade teacher *extraordinaire*. Our own children benefited from her rare talent as a teacher. We were on opposing sides in this decision, but not on opposing sides in the one church of Christ we both confess each time we speak the Apostle's Creed. Near her was Elfrieda Miller, whose eyes were filled with tears but whose voice was steady as she took my hand in hers and assured me that her opposition to the withdrawal was not opposition to me personally. We embraced and spoke words which reassured us both of our oneness in Christ.

Finally the time came for us to leave. I don't recall the hour. Beverly and I found our way to our parsonage door at a late hour, tired to be sure, but grateful that we could see this hour and experience it with a congregation we love and admire so much.

CHAPTER 2

An Evangelical Way of Life

Three quarters of a century of experience and tradition in Grace Church lay behind the eventful evening of September 20, 1977. The contours of that experience, marked by significant landmarks and milestones in the congregation's journey are traceable and help explain why the congregation took the step it did.

Two years after the turn of the present century a group of families living in the prairie fields just west of Chicago established Grace Evangelical Lutheran Church. The place was known as Harlem, an unincorporated section of Oak Park. The date was March 17, 1902. Five years earlier, however, these Lutherans of German background put up a one room frame building to serve as a branch Lutheran school connected with their home congregation, St. John's Lutheran Church in Forest Park, Ill. Lutheran day schools were a strong part of the Missouri Synod Lutheran tradition in America. More than any other Protestant group in the wave of 19th century immigrants, the German Lutherans who formed the Missouri Synod in 1839 in Perry County, Missouri, put major stress on the establishing of schools to teach their children the Christian faith, give them a sound elementary education, as well as preserve for them the German language and cultural heritage that were intertwined with Luther's Small Catechism. It has been a noteworthy element in the remarkable cohesiveness that has marked congregations which chose to affiliate with the Missouri Synod.

The families living in the Harlem neighborhood built their

school in 1897, and received permission to found their own congregation five years later because of the inconvenience of walking from Harlem to the St. John's congregation twice on Sundays—once for Sunday morning worship and then returning in the afternoon for the confirmation instruction of children.

In 1904 the members erected an imposing church building on the corner of Augusta and Belleforte in Oak Park. The congregation grew, but not without particular growing pains associated with a cluster of German-speaking families struggling with the sizeable issues of assimilation into American life while retaining the Christian way of life as Lutherans practiced it.

Another important feature of Grace Church's earlier decades was the inclusion of faculty members and families from nearby Concordia Teachers College. The presence of these Christians was indeed a blessing in the parish. Mixed in with the blessing were the inevitable problems of towngown relationships. Wrestling with these concerns consumed much of the energies and positive spirit of the first three pastors of the congregation. The third in the series, Rev. H. C. Engelbrecht, was a particularly thoughtful individual whose time of service at Grace overlapped the World War I years. The head-on encounters of factions within the congregation was too much for Engelbrecht. He left in 1922, a man broken in mind and spirit. His subsequent career as a writer is memorable for his having coined the phrase "the merchants of death" for the financiers who backed the Nazi leaders in the 1940's.

In 1922 a new era for the parish began with the arrival of Otto Geiseman as pastor. He had reacted strongly against the heavy-handed strain of Germanic legalism which was part of the Missouri Synod tradition, and had very nearly given up the pastoral vocation before he was ordained and on his way in ministry in downstate Illinois. But he had hung on, and learned the requirements of keeping an *evangelical* spirit uppermost in carrying out his calling as a Lutheran pastor.

The term *evangelical* has a unique, all-important quality in understanding the best of the Lutheran heritage as it came to flower in the congregation as the years progressed.

Evangelical means Gospel-centered. That is the opposite of Law-centered. Evangelical does not mean the repudiation of the Law of God in the belief and practices of parishioners. According to the Lutheran accent in theology, the Law (expressed essentially in the Ten Commandments) is the Word of God's judgment revealing to us our sins. The Law mirrors our transgressions, curbs our willfulness as imperfect Christians, and holds before us the holy will of God for the direction of our lives. But the Law does not and cannot rescue us from our plight, nor is the Law the motive for loving God and neighbor. Law-oriented religion breeds fear and stirs guilt. Building on the Law heads to pride and the inclination to exclude other believers from the fellowship. It creates an atmosphere of legalism and heavy-handedness, not because the Law itself is evil but because the inclination of the human heart is to put the traditions and practices and precepts of humans on par with the precepts of God.

The evangelical way in congregation life draws upon the Gospel of God's full, liberating love revealed to the world in Jesus Christ, the crucified and risen Lord. With the Gospel as the center, the whole range of Christian doctrine and practice is related to that center as the petals of a rose fan out from the bud at its heart. The way of the Gospel, the evangelical spirit, keeps the emphasis upon God's love as the power to belong to Him in faith and to others in love. The evangelical spirit keeps people caring and forgiving of each other in the congregation; it leads people to see the difference between the traditions of human origin and the living Word of God which the Bible speaks to us. The evangelical way in the congregation keeps people open to embrace new directions into which the Holy Spirit leads, while holding fast the fundamentals of the Biblical faith which unite the parishioners with the people of God of all time and all places on earth.

Such generalized descriptions of the evangelical faith have profound and practical implications for pastor and people in the congregation setting. Under the pastoral leadership of Otto Geiseman, the evangelical tone and direction that was latent in Grace Church took on new life. English replaced German as the dominant language of the parish (a transition accomplished neither quickly nor easily). Geiseman began doing new things for that time, even shocking things! He made mission calls on people with non-German background and did not hesitate to join groups in the community which brought him into contact with the business and professional leaders of the western suburbs of Chicago. He also continued his professional education with graduate studies at a nearby seminary of another Lutheran synod and earned his doctorate in theology—with the blessing and the encouragement of the congregation behind him. As a man endowed with splendid personal qualities of strength as pastor, preacher, and counselor, he met some long-standing conflicts within the congregation with an even-handed directness. Upon receiving his first anonymous hate letter from a sick-minded person of the congregation, he brought the letter to the next Sunday's service, read it aloud, and stated his willingness to resign on the spot if a *single* parishioner of Grace Church would stand up in the public assembly and support its contents. No one did. Although the poison-pen letters did not cease altogether from that point on, the writers knew they would get nowhere with those tactics which had been harassing enough to drive off the previous several pastors as spiritually crippled men. As the congregation grew in the 1920's, the growth was internal in the evangelical spirit of the Christian faith as well as external in numbers.

By 1928 it was evident that the present church and school were not adequate, and after a lengthy series of negotiations with the Synodical fathers in St. Louis, the congregation bought land on the square block of Concordia Teachers College in River Forest and erected a stately Gothic church building and school facility. A land contract was signed by the congregation and Synod in 1928 when Grace Church bought two acres of land from the Synod. To that we return in a later chapter.

But at this point in the story, we do well to appreciate the enormous task the congregation undertook in just holding on to, not to mention systematically paying for the costly church and school that was dedicated in February, 1931—the heart of the Great Depression. It is no small commentary on the generous stewardship of giving the evangelical way in the church creates to note that the property and church building was paid for sixteen years later.

In the post World War II years the complexion of Grace Church became more distinct. Its evangelical contours became more pronounced. In 1947 one of the parishioners, Paul Weiss, saw that the work of the pastorate was more than Dr. Geiseman could handle alone. He appreciated the fact that the entire congregation had just concluded a demanding financial venture of paying for the church, so instead of asking the parish to add more dollars to the budget for a regular assistant pastor, he put up the needed money himself for an assistant to the pastor. Geiseman was quick to see the possibilities of such a large-hearted offer, and the system was underway which brought to Grace Church seminary graduates for a two year period of ordained pastoral work coupled with the incentive toward additional growth in the profession of ministry through graduate study at any one of the universities and seminaries in the Chicago area. Such an arrangement reflected a breadth of vision on the part of parishioniers and pastor, and that is part of an evangelical spirit which opens people up to the world without turning them into worldly people. The dozen men who have served as assistants to the pastor since the late 1940's have gone on to significant careers. James Manz, Kenneth Breimeier, Martin Marty and Richard Gotsch are among the known and respected clergy now serving in widely varying ministries. Each can look back upon the Grace Church years with appreciation for the *spirit* of the congregation which has made its lasting impression upon them.

Strange though it sounds, the evangelical spirit given to Grace congregation often brought it into sharp conflict with the Missouri Synod leadership as well as other congregation and pastors. The idea of an assistant to the pastor, called for a two year period with built-in graduate work encouragement, was anathema to many Missouri Synod clergy for whom this was a new idea. The very fact that the Grace people built the size and quality of church and school in spite of the depression odds against them stirred jealousy in some who tended to think of Grace as a silk-stocking operation in a plush suburb where the ushers wore formal morning coats in Sunday Service, the pastor actually wore a turned-around collar which was identified with popish antics, and the chinaware at church dinners was not cheap. River Forest is a plush suburb. The pastor did depart from the sacrosanct black gown and black tie. The church dinners were served on quality chinaware, on linen tablecloths, and with saucers under the coffee cups! And all this was without apology. It was the sign of people learning more and more, as Pastor Geiseman put it so often, to do everything in the congregation with our best, not our least.

In 1945 the congregation faced its first major test in its relationship to the leadership of the Missouri Synod. The issue was the evangelical way to church life in conflict with a legalistic direction. Otto Geiseman has been among the leaders of a group of pastors, missionaries, and professors of the Synod which issued a documented entitled "A Statement". It was signed by forty four clergy and addressed to the leadership of the Synod, appealing for Christ's love to prevail in matters connected with prayer fellowship, unity with other Lutherans, and less cocksureness in the way in which Bible passages were interpreted to pass judgment on and remain isolated from Christians not of the Missouri Synod. The publication of the Statement caused a storm of reaction throughout the Synod, so that finally the signers withdrew the document at the request of Synodical President John Behnken. The point in withdrawing it was not to repudiate its contents but to acquiesce in the administration's request to get these issues into the districts and circuits of the Synod in the administration's manner. The issues never really received the attention intended through the official channels, but the effect of the Statement was powerful nonetheless. It served to open a two-decade era of unprecedented flowering of the evangelical spirit in the Missouri Synod. The high water mark of the consequences of the Statement issued in 1945 was the Missouri Synod's adopting of the Mission Affirmations at the Synodical Convention in Detroit in 1965, which affirmed the basic evangelical spirit in relation to issues raised by Geiseman and others in the mid 1940's, as well as expanding the Christian mission at home and abroad.

Geiseman had the full support of Grace congregation as he exercised a leadership role in the formulating and advocating *A Statement.* It was essential to him that he not proceed alone, without the understanding and the support of the parish. The Church Council and the Voter's Assembly were on record in their backing of the very things which Grace Church stood for as a congregation. This made Dr. Geiseman's role much more than an assertion of his personal convictions; it was a reflection of the will and spirit of the congregation. Although the facing of that issue meant the loss of some members who felt strongly enough about it to withdraw and transfer to other congregations, it also brought some members to Grace Church precisely because of the stand taken by the people.

It has always been easy to identify an evangelical spirit with a permissive spirit, as though centering the congregation's life in the love of Christ could be translated to mean that anything goes. But that equation was more often assumed than proven! A distinctive mark from communicant membership of Missouri Synod parish practice was the exclusion of members who professed active participation in the religious rites of the Masonic Lodge. There was no absolute uniformity on this measure, but the prevailing assumption was that no lodge members were accepted as full communicant members. On one occasion in the early 1950's a delegation of irate pastors and parishioners from other Missouri Synod congregations descended on Geiseman and the Grace Church elders demanding to know why Grace tolerates "all those lodge members" as everyone seemed to know. Geiseman asked them to name some of the "everyone" alleged to know about the scandalous permissiveness at Grace Church. No one seemed to know an "anyone" among the "everyone". Then, Pastor Geiseman continued, surely the delegation could take a Grace membership list and begin naming the lodge members. Could just one example be cited, and then that would suffice for all the others purportedly smuggled into the flock? No one could name a single lodge member, because it happened to be the evangelical way at Grace to point out to prospective members our conviction: the Gospel as the way to God's heart and not the way of man's works to win Divine approval. Grace Church makes that point in its ministry, then and now. Evangelical does not mean the spurious kind of tolerance which takes nothing seriously and therefore accepts anything. It is the conviction that since God Himself takes us with the seriousness of the cross, all things are made new in the power of His love. Standing against something does not leave us anti-people, crotchety and mean spirited, but strong in the desire to show what does and what does not grow from the Gospel.

The evangelical way in congregation life equips one to keep his sense of humor intact, especially when the heat is on. Martin Marty was a newly ordained assistant at Grace in 1952, when Dr. Geiseman was the target of incessant accusation from his Missouri Synod pastoral colleagues for his position advocating prayer with other Lutherans and Christians, closer ties of Lutheran unity, and moving the church much more into the world as a witness for mission. Otto Geiseman had once told a group of carping clergy that there was nothing wrong with them that reading a new book and getting their pants pressed would not help. Sentences with that sting have a way of being remembered! In any case, Geiseman was for the umpteenth time on the firing line. Young Pastor Marty was getting his baptism of fire in pastoral conferences as the Grace assistant, and was mildly shocked by the vehemence of the charges and accusations against his boss. Wanting to ease the atmosphere in the room as the clergy kept up the barrage, he lit a cigar. Geiseman noted that and shortly thereafter penciled a note on a slip of paper and folded it discreetly, then asked that it be passed to his assistant at the opposite end of the table. The preachers on the attack of course assumed that this was strategy advice from the old pro to the rookie. Marty opened the note and read: "You lit the wrong end". The second-most distasteful sound to the Devil is sanctified laughter, and when a person is secure in Christ there are openings for that good sound in the most unexpected places.

My own first day at Grace Church was an introduction to the evangelical way in an episode I will cherish all my days. I had completed my seminary training in June of 1954, and accepted the call to come to Grace for the two year assistantship. I was single, and carried all I owned in two suitcases from the Sante Fe station in Chicago where Pastor Geiseman met me. We chatted about things of surface importance while driving from the old Dearborn Street station out Washington Boulevard in Chicago to the Graemere Hotel, then a jewel of Chicago's west side hotels. The maitre-de was a Grace parishioner, Don Eckdahl, and I had the distinct feeling of being welcomed in gracious taste as we had our breakfast in the understated elegance of the Graemere dining room. Then on to Grace Church at the corner of Bonnie Brae and Division in River Forest, and a good long look at the granite and Gothic architecture of the building which has been "home" in my pastoral vocation since. The first man we met in the parking lot was the Mr. Grace Church of that day, Chris Garbers. This white haired patriarchal figure met me with an immediate warmth of spirit that I had sensed in Otto Geiseman as well. One can tell something about a congregation by meeting the laity who are around the church on a Saturday morning! Mr. Garbers had dropped in to check over whatever work may have collected during the week in the church office that he might help with. He had served in all the major offices, and had been chairman of the building committee of Grace Church in 1931. He was a grocery-man by trade, and had built a flourishing business in wholesale foods over the years. Yet here was no pseudo-sophisticated suburbanite who built his financial kingdom by crushing as many heads as that took to get ahead. He was a modest man, unpretentious, not requiring a show of wealth in order to make an impression. When Jesus spoke of the "salt of the earth" He was describing people like Chris Garbers, whose hearts were home for the Spirit's dwelling. It was a nice touch that Pastor Geiseman suggested Mr. Garbers show me around the building initially, while he tended to some pastoral item that was waiting for him after fetching me from the railroad station. The church belonged to God's people, not the pastor. After a quick tour I was back at the pastor's study door, and the first of so many happy, instructive hours at Grace Church began.

Geiseman sat me down in the chair across the desk from where he sat, and offered me a cigar (the wrong end of which I would probably have lit, too). My refusal was not so much because I didn't smoke cigars but because of a slight edge of nervousness about how all this was really going to go. Dr. Geiseman paused a moment, then looked me squarely in the eye and said, "Dean, there is one thing I want you to get straight from day one at Grace Church". I was not totally taken aback by that opening sentence, sensing that the brand new seminary graduate might well be advised early on that he would not be expected to rearrange either the universe or the congregation in his two year stint now beginning. But Pastor Geiseman had no such speech. Instead, his next sentence was: "We're not doing the Lord's work around here as best it ought be done . . . and whatever ideas, whatever creative imagination, whatever energies you can bring to our parish family, it's welcome and it's needed."

As I think back now on that opening conversation I marvel at it. It turned out to be not just rhetoric designed to put a new partner at ease (in lieu of a cigar). He meant it. There *were* some ideas and some hopes and some dreams that I brought with me from my seminary training and my vicarage years in Europe and Japan. I was encouraged to offer them, to test them out with the pastoral and parish leadership, and to apply them in the rich blend of congregation life at Grace into which I was so grateful to enter.

An example of how this worked was in parish mission outreach.

A key insight into the New Testament image of the congregation in mission is the sentence from Ephesians 4 which speaks of the laity as the primary arm of mission outreach. It is all too common to leave that to clergy. But if ministry can also be understood as the faith of the laity at work in daily life, then the outreach of the congregation is fully orbed instead of limited to what the minister does as one person. The time at Grace was ripe for that accent to become operational. As time passed, the lay leaders of the various men's, women's and young adult organizations of the congregation accepted a new feature in the meetings and work of their meetings and planning sessions. It meant some brief time in each group for the names and addresses of new people in the neighborhood who had no known Christian affiliation to be made available to fellow members who might live nearby or have some other point of common contact with the newcomers. Another period of time was given to the things which parishioners learn by this experience of outreach themselves. Underneath it all is the most powerful aspect of the evangelical way of congregation life, that the members of the congregation exist for the sake of those who have not yet come to the Faith! Not all of us see this clearly, of course. But as this elemental premise of mission takes a deeper hold, the entire spirit and direction of the congregation is influenced positively. The familiar pitfalls of ingrown, self-serving attitudes do not throw people off the main track. The parish agenda is spared the blight of trivia. Worship takes on deeper meaning as the most central act of our life and faith together. The right kind of criteria are given prominence to help us establish our priorities and utilize our resources.

From my first day at Grace, I knew the joy of ministry, which is the joy of joining the People of God in the ministry of Christ Himself as He is present among us through the Holy Spirit.

Where the Gospel is uppermost in the congregation, relationships show it. As powerful a leader as Dr. Geiseman was, he nevertheless sought to respect the opinions of colleagues and parishioners and not rule by the sheer force of personality. The Church Council at Grace is a working group of three elders, three trustees, three financial officers, the treasurer, three members of the youth council, and various staff members from the faculty of the school. The Council meets monthly, and in twenty four years of attending meetings of the Council I cannot recall a single outburst of uncontrolled rancor. Dr. Geiseman's style was to deal directly with controversial issues, but to ask for the views of each Council member person by person around the circle to begin forming a base of shared opinion leading to consensus. An opposing view is not to be ridiculed but listened to, and matters come to a vote only after the Council itself is satisfied that enough discussion has taken place. This strong collegial style of administration took on even more importance in the turbulent years of the 1960's and '70's, when Grace struggled to apply its evangelical spirit to the explosive problems of racial strife and the Vietnam War.

Otto Geiseman had envisioned a phasing of shared pastoral duties between himself and me following my acceptance of the call to serve as associate pastor in 1959. We were one year along in a program whereby more and more responsibility in the pastorate would shift to my side when cancer surgery became necessary for him in 1960. His recovery from the removal of one lung was excellent. In 1962 the congregation marked his 40th anniversary of pastoral service at Grace Church by sending him and Mrs. Geiseman on a tour of congregations and church work around the world. He lectured at pastoral conferences and preached in Lutheran pulpits in Japan and Korea, Taiwan and Hong Kong, India, the Holy Land, and northern Europe. Members contributed to a special fund for his dispensing to meet particular needs as he became acquainted with them in various parts of the world. It was a magnificent experience for the Geisemans, and helped to build closer ties with Grace and Christian communities in the Far East and India. Following his return from the three month journey, however, the malignancy causing the removal of his lung came back to him. He battled what became a terminal disease from spring till fall in 1962, and died in the peace of Christ on November 7, 1962.

The congregation's memorial to his ministry was not only a tribute to Pastor Geiseman's faithful work over four decades. It was also a commentary on the manner in which the inner growth in spiritual stature had taken root in the membership. The Kingdom Frontiers program, as it was called, was established as the Dr. O. A. Geiseman Memorial. It provided members the opportunity to contribute to a special Kingdom Frontiers Fund in the congregation, directed by three elected Board members and devoted to support of fledgling mission ventures at home and abroad which did not yet have institutional support but which showed promise. The particular feature of the program was to link Grace Church members with the world and the church beyond the boundaries of the congregation, whether near or far. Under the auspices of the Kingdom Frontiers program, high school youth have spent summers working on an Indian Reservation in northeastern Arizona, seminarians have worked under black pastoral leadership on Chicago's west side, a young couple of the congregation have served homeless children in a Christian school in Florence, Italy, urban ministries in the bohemia of Chicago's north side have been given grants, an Indian national pastor from Bombay came to Grace congregation for a year's activity on our staff, a Biblical exegete—also a Grace member—was sent to Lae, New Guinea for a year's special service in the all-Lutheran seminary there, the beginnings of the highly promising Chicago Uptown Ministry were supported by the Kingdom Frontiers Fund, and for the past two years a senior missionary theologian of the Lutheran Church has been supported full time in his teaching vocation at Concordia Seminary, Hong Kong. Over the past 15 years, Grace members have contributed several hundreds of thousands of dollars toward people in the ministry near and far. It continues to be a major source for the enlightened lay participation in the world Christian mission, with the reminder that the world is as close as River Forest and as distant as the southern tip of India or the central highlands of New Guinea.

A similar congregation program that reflects the outgoing, progressive evangelical spirit of the congregation is the memorial program established by Harold and Dorothy Garbers in memory of their son, William, who died while preparing to be a Lutheran teacher. The William Garbers Memorial sends Grace School faculty members to other Christian communities abroad or in the U. S. A. for the purpose of broadening the faculty member's horizon as well as bringing the benefits of that person's experience to bear upon Christians who welcome it in their work. Thus, the school principal, Victor Waldschmidt, spent a half year as consultant to the Seoul International School in Seoul, Korea, in 1969, and traveled to the Arab Lutheran School of the Lutheran Church of the Redeemer in Jerusalem in 1978. Paul Bouman has spent time among church musicians in Wesphalia, W. Germany. Margaret Kruse and Lyle Mortensen have conducted special learning and teaching tours in the Atlantic States and New England area.

Lois Nielsen and Betty Moser have spent a summer visiting primary grades in British schools, both learning and sharing their experiences as Grace teachers. The program has also brought into Grace Church and School gifted educators from overseas, especially from the Orient and from India.

So it is that the outward reach and inward growth of the congregation has been quietly and steadily increasing. Along with spiritual soundness the goal of excellence in ministry has been one which members and staff have sought to help each other reach.

The music side of the congregation has shown this with

wide-ranging influence. Martin Lochner and Carl Halter, organists and music directors of the congregation in the 1930's set high standards of musical excellence which the present minister of music, Mr. Paul Bouman, has extended.

Music becomes a way of life at Grace very early. In what outsiders have described with understandable envy but in a smiling fashion as "the farm system," the children of Grace School begin receiving formal choir training at the fifth grade and continue through the eighth. This provides a yearly supply of youngsters entering high school years, and the High School Choir of the congregation, with an excellent foundation in choral training. The Senior Choir, in turn, shows results of well-trained young men and women entering its membership after years of experience from the fifth grade onward.

Over the past eight years the Grace Senior Choir has taken the lead in presenting eight Bach Cantatas during the fall, winter, and spring. Each Sunday afternoon cantata includes a guest organist, instrumentalists, and a guest preacher to preach the homily that accompanies the cantata. The response has brought people from throughout the Chicago area and beyond, who are glad to travel some distances on Sunday afternoon to hear the best of the Lutheran musical heritage sung and spoken by gifted musicians who are—all of them—faithful parishioners who sing and play not for a fee but as a part of their membership at Grace. Instrumentalists of the congregation include exceptionally skilled professional musicians who are members of the Chicago Symphony, but they—like plumbers, electricians, accountants, teachers, nurses and doctors and parishioners from all walks of life contribute their talents for the good of all. It is all part of the evangelical way of life that makes the word Grace more than a name for the congregation. It describes the power of Christ's love to bring a people of such wide diversity together and hold them on course in mission to the community and world.

Festival Services at Grace, particularly at Easter and on Christmas Eve, bring Christians from many other congregations to Grace Church to hear the music and the message which gives the parish life. It is particularly rewarding for teachers in the parish school to see graduates of previous years returning to participate in holiday worship as they remember it earlier in their own lives.

Speaking of teachers, Grace Lutheran School is an enormously important part of our total ministry. Serving children from kindergarten through the eighth grade, some 275 of them each school day of the year is a high calling indeed. Victor Waldschmidt, our Grace Lutheran School principal, has been leading the school program since the late 1940's. I had always admired him and found him a splendid colleague, but that appreciation truly deepened in the years following 1963 and my assuming the full pastoral leadership of the congregation. The wisdom, cooperation, and competence Victor Waldschmidt shared freely with me as a fellow member of the Grace staff has been another major reason why serving at Grace is a joy. Week by week throughout the year we gather for early Wednesday morning worship together as a staff. How good it is when the words of Christ that we speak together in worship carry over to define our relationships as we carry out our individual tasks during the day! Grace Lutheran School has been a strong and positive Christian influence in so many young lives throughout this century. All of us in the congregation support it; we all care greatly about its continuance as an arm of Christian witness and nurture in the lives of children and their families.

I would hope that every congregational staff senses the importance of putting the message of the Gospel into practice in staff attitudes and relationships. Parishioners need to see that demonstrated. It is part of the integrity of witness which pastors and teachers owe the congregation. Especially vital to it all is our life of worship together, both in staff and congregation. Our worship life is our glue. It holds us together like nothing else. At Grace we are well glued indeed! There are so many people with gifts to share and the underlying spirit of Christ motivates us to share them in love.

This profile of the character of a congregation is not complete without acknowledgment of our sins, our faults, our shortcomings which are not difficult to spot. Our ministry to public school youth, those who do not have their elementary schooling in the parish school, is a particular challenge and we have much growing to do in this area. Although Grace Church has been home base for a fellowship of older, single adults from several dozen congregations over the past ten years, the overall ministry to older single adults is another aspect of our work where we are lacking. I hear of other congregations that hold meaningful retreats for individuals and families; we have never been able to do that effectively and we have much to learn about it. The manner in which we have dealt with conflicts is one in which we could hardly claim full competence. Whenever some member, any member, is neglected or forgotten we are reminded of our failures. In my files is a letter from an articulate member who took the time and the trouble to point out to me that the main impression he received as a Grace member was that we were interested only in his pocketbook. I have kept that letter as a reminder to me that after a congregation and pastor have done their best, there is no sitting back to admire ourselves. There are always the missed persons, the people who are not heard or reached as they should be. We live by grace in order to be Grace Church, and because God Himself is infinitely patient and merciful to us, we have hope and courage.

Here, then, is a composite profile of a congregation's coming into its own as a community of Christians who are together because they want to be together, bonded in Christ's love and blessed by His Spirit in order to nurture each other in faith and bring the witness to those who do not yet know how broad and deep and high is the redeeming love of God in Christ Jesus. Some 1750 comprise the Grace family. We have particular blessings, just as every congregation on earth. Ours are all centered in the Gospel which is preached, creative fellowship, and partnership with God's people nearby as well as at distant corners of the earth. Fifty years ago the congregation came upon an eight word motto which serves well as a rainbow over our life then and now: "Our Aim—Save Souls. Our Means—the Gospel." Understanding soul-saving in the Biblical sense of giving our whole lives to God—body and soul and mind—we have come to our present from a rich and diverse past. It is good, very good, to be part of God's People at Grace Church.

Chapter 3

Denomination Versus Congregation

It was an unusual place, an unusual day, and an unusual letter. On July 20, 1969, late in the morning, I was standing in the Roman theater in the ancient ruins of Caesarea along the Mediterranaean seashore in Israel. Beverly and I were in the Holy Land for that month, touring with a group of journalists and teachers under the auspices of the America-Israel Cultural Foundation. Someone in our group had a portable radio along, making it possible for us to join most of the family of mankind in listening to Neil Armstrong's words as he set foot on the moon. With my ears I was listening to that epochal event.

With my eyes I was learning of another eventful shift in another, lesser-known universe which did, however, mean a great deal to me and the congregation I served. My pastoral assistant back home, Philip Bruening, wrote to me of the unexpected turn of events at the Denver Convention of the Missouri Synod. The incumbent, Oliver Harms, had been unseated in an unprecedented action of strong political maneuvering by the ultra-conservative wing of the Synod. Harms, who was a conservative churchman with an evenhanded evangelical touch in his style of leadership, had maintained his customary cool during the months preceding the convention. But not his opponents in the Synod. The Missouri Synod had long had its right-wing voice in unofficial publications such as "The Confessional Lutheran" which dated back to the 1940's. But the movement of the far right took on momentum after 1965. These people did their political homework with a diligence most of the rest of us missed or did not take seriously in the four years following.

Their man was Jacob Preus, a traveler between Synods and one around whom controversy always had gathered. His experiences of discontent and his accusations against the spiritual soundness of faculty and administrative leaders in the former Evangelical Lutheran Church should have been more carefully noted by Missourians. His reputation in Missouri had been known chiefly in connection with his leadership role in the next Synod to which he belonged, the tiny and ultra-conversative, Norwegian-oriented Evangelical Lutheran Synod. Preus, together with his brother, Robert, had led the way in breaking fellowship with the Missouri Synod in 1955. Then, suddenly and without explanation, he joined the Missouri Synod in 1958 as a faculty member at Concordia Seminary, Springfield, Ill., and in 1962 became its president. From that position he exercised his influence as an aggressive contender for restoring the Missouri Synod to his version of conservatism, a version which was shared widely enough with fellow pastors and lay delegates at Denver to win the presidential election and to unseat an incumbent president for the first time in Missouri Synod history.

This was the problematic news of the letter I read in the Caearean theater, and as I looked at that stage where so many ancient dramas had been enacted and political speeches heard, I wondered what this new politics and new drama meant in the denomination in which I was a member and Grace Church was one of 6000 affiliated congregations.

The other part of the Convention report was surprising, too.

Although the delegates had elected an arch-conservative to the denominational presidency, they had then voted approval for pulpit and altar fellowship with the American Lutheran Church. It has often been noted that the Missouri Synod had a fascinating kind of unpredictability about itself, and the Denver convention was further documentation. The sanctioning of exchanging pulpits and the opening of communion altars for parishioners of LCMS and ALC congregations was consistent with the evangelical movement in Missouri all along. The Preus election was a victory for the opposite branch of the Synodical family. So, no one went home from Denver with all the trophies, and every thoughtful delegate came home scratching his head in wonderment and curious to see what would happen now.

Grace congregation received a vivid, personal report on the Denver actions of the denomination from Walter Christopher, a lay delegate to the meeting. This life-long member of the congregation, and experienced attorney with forty years experience in the sometimes rough-and-tumble aspects of seeking justice in the civil court was both shocked and outraged by the unabashed politicking he had witnessed prior to and during the Denver convention. He said so bluntly.

That summary meeting in the Fellowship Hall of the church on a warm August evening in 1969 was much more than a convention report. It was the first step on a lengthy, demanding, exasperating, and wonderful journey for Grace Church.

Most of the members had read the newspaper accounts of the Missouri Convention, so the decisions of the convention were not necessary to recount. What members were anxious to probe was the story under the story. How could it happen that the staid, conventional, unflappable clergy and laity of the Missouri Synod could turn in such a Janus-headed performance in voting Harms out and Preus in and at the same meeting put forth the hand of spiritual fellowship to another branch of Lutherans? There were no easy answers. But there was spirited discussion.

For the first time there was the faintest sign on the horizon that the fiery controversy which had split the Denver convention very nearly down the middle would make its way into the congregation—and ours was not the only congregation receiving such early warning signals.

The Missouri Synod differs from many, if not most other major Lutheran denominations as well as from Roman Catholics, Episcopalians, Methodists, and Presbyterians in that it is decidedly congregational in its relationship to congregations. The congregation is not, according to the constitution, under the hierarchy of the Synod. It is under the Holy Scriptures, as confessed in the Lutheran Reformation writings which place the Gospel of Christ front and center in all doctrinal belief and church actions. The key phrase in the Missouri Synod constitution is Article VII:

> "In its relation to its members the Synod is not an ecclesiastical government exercising legislative or coercive powers, and with respect to the individual congregation's right of self-government it is but an advisory body. Accordingly no resolution of the Synod imposing anything upon the individual congregation is of binding force if it is not in accordance with the Word of God or if it is inexpedient as far as the condition of a congregation is concerned."

This meant that congregations were free to accept or reject the Denver resolution on pulpit and altar fellowship, and the Synod could not do anything more than offer the convention actions to each congregation for approval or for rejection.

Grace Church chose to act upon the resolution to join hands spiritually with ALC Christians. To people outside of the Lutheran tradition such a decision must seem inconsequential indeed. But for parishioners who had longed all their lifetime to express outwardly the inner spiritual unity which is Christ-given and not man-made, the prospect of having an ALC preacher stand in our pulpit or the prospect of their kneeling at the altar of an ALC congregation and communing with ALC Christians was not anything casual. It marked the fulfillment of years of prayers, hopes, and dreams.

That moment came on the last Sunday in September following the July decision in 1969. Pastor Wayne Tellekson, minister of the United Lutheran Church, accepted our invitation to preach at Grace. He stepped into the pulpit, announced his text, and an expectant hush fell upon the congregation. With something of a sigh of appreciation, he spoke his first sentence: "It's about time." There was an instant wave of approving response, almost applause! that swept through the members. A new era was underway, one which would bring Grace congregation closer to its Lutheran neighboring parish than ever before. My turn came the following Sunday to preach and commune at United. That day was over a century in coming, and it rejoiced my heart to see so many Grace members kneeling at the altar at United. Surely this sight is good in God's sight, for had not His Son prayed so earnestly on the night before Calvary that we might all be one, even as the Father and He are one? (John 17:21).

But the joyful experiences of new and enlarged spiritual ties of Lutheran unity on the home front were tempered by problems looming on the Synodical level. President Preus had sacked Dr. Richard Jungkuntz, his former faculty colleague at Springfield and the chairman of the Synod's Commission on Theology and Church Relations. Jungkuntz was the quality of evangelical Lutheran theologians who had the respect of so many of us, but not all of us in the clergy ranks of the Synod. No reason for his discontinuance was given, and when I heard of it late in the spring of 1970 it occurred to me that here was a brother out of a job with little more than a few week's notice.

Word of this had come to me from a report on a pastoral meeting in Michigan which had registered concern over the action. Rev. Bertwin Frey, pastor of Messiah Lutheran Church in the suburbs of Cleveland had expressed his conviction that something constructive must be done, and done soon for Richard Jungkuntz. I contacted Frey, with word of my interest in acting upon his suggestion. We discussed the matter by phone and letter, agreeing to do two things.

First, we would write to as many clergy as both of us knew in the Synod, appealing for an emergency support fund for Jungkuntz to be paid for summer school teaching he could do at Concordia Seminary, St. Louis, Mo.

In the same mailing we included a statement entitled "A Declaration of Intention" in which we asked brother pastors to add their signatures of support for the following measures, which were an appeal for evangelical rather than legalistic Synodical leadership.

I had brought these matters to the attention of our Board of Elders before acting upon them personally, remembering the example Otto Geiseman had set back in the mid-1940's. Going off into the Synodical wars by myself was little more than irresponsible foolishness. I was called to serve and to lead a congregation, and with the partnership and support of the congregation the cause could be worthwhile. Our people not only supported the spirit of the effort Frey and I were initiating, but opened Grace Church as a channel for contributions for Professor Jungkuntz and his family support.

1215 signatures were gathered, representing approximately 20% of the clergy roster of the Synod. With that list of names in hand, Pastor Frey and I made our way to St. Louis to keep an appointment with Synodical president, Jacob Preus. It was our judgment that the meeting might have more substance if we came bearing the sentiment of a significant number of fellow clergy, rather than making it merely our own personal concern. President Preus received us on a spring morning in May, 1970, and heard us out. Instead of offering much actual response to our plea for Jungkuntz and an evangelical style of relationships with brother clergy, he suggested that we both return in a week and present our materials to the Board of Directors of the Synod who would be meeting in St. Louis seven days hence. We explained that we were traveling on our own expense, and that time and air fare did not make that our first choice. We preferred leaving our message and the signatures with him, and asking him to do with it whatever he thought appropriate. He persisted in his request, however, that we both come back in person. To that we agreed.

I shall not forget the meeting with the Synodical Board that took place on schedule. The arrangement in the room made it immediately clear to me where Frey and I stood. Preus and the Board members had seats around a large board room table. Frey and Lueking were placed outside that circle, so that I stared at the back of the head of one of the directors throughout the meeting. Preus began the session with a rather tense, accusatory statement, indicating that our action of seeking and finding 1200 signers to a statement of intention was in his judgment a divisive act. Then followed an obviously rehearsed series of speeches supporting the president and taking issue with us. In fact, the Board members each had a file document unknown to Frey or me. It consisted of copies of my personal letters and memos sent out in quest of support for Jungkuntz! I did not regard these as top secret documents by any means, but I took a very dim view indeed of Synodical leaders gathering my personal materials without my knowledge or consent and putting me through several hours of intense questioning on *how* the document came to be assembled and the signers contacted, rather than a single word of attention to the content of the appeal. Was I in the company of spiritual brothers or the CIA? Later it saddened me but made me wiser to learn that the materials the Board of Directors had received from President Preus had been sent from my own office by our church secretary, who subsequently resigned and left our congregation.

It was sobering, yet educational for me and for our Council to learn of such things. I resolved, however, not to make mention of this to our congregation members and certainly not to give it an airing from the pulpit. My decision was to hold back actions that were that distant from the way Christians belong to each other, even in the face of sharp disagreements. Perhaps I should have laid everything out in the open from the start, trusting our members to be able to accept it without being so offended as to abandon the whole business in disgust. Where and how does one draw the line in choosing what to share and what to simply hold in the heart and go on with more important things? I had kept the elders informed at every step, and they were immensely helpful and supportive. That was enough.

Our days together as Grace congregation were much too filled with other urgent demands. These were the long, hot summers of racial riots, and as the west side of Chicago went up in flames I was more interested in securing Grace parishioners to volunteer their homes in our suburban areas for frightened black adults and children who are always the most direct victims of racial violence. These were the years of growing unrest over our involvement as a nation in Vietnam, and my interest lay more with our 18 year old young men and their families facing the draft issue than bothering them with ecclesiastical pranks.

But the controversy gripping the Synod would not go away by ignoring it, and the network of contact with several thousand clergy which Pastor Frey and I initiated became a continuing form of advocacy of the evangelical spirit among pastors and laity from coast to coast. Other clergy in the Synod began similar efforts of protest as the lengthened list of professors, staff workers in Synodical offices, and missionaries who left their ministries because of harassment or were simply terminated without cause given for their release. Pastor Richard Koenig began a newsletter from his Amherst, Mass., church office, which reached a wide number of Synodical members who asked for it. Pastor Omar Stuenkel in Cleveland, Ohio, organized a smaller group of pastors for the purpose of raising awareness of what was going on in the Synod and mobilizing opposition to the direction which seemed to be a 180 degree turn from the evangelical flowering in the Synod from the mid 1940's onward. None of us chose these activities with thoughts of becoming political kingmakers in the Synod. And the near total political predominance of the arch-conservatives in the Synod in subsequent conventions would have made us all run for cover if we entertained serious thoughts of "taking over" the Synod as we felt it had been assaulted by those who had effectively moved into every office of influence to which one can be elected in the Missouri Synod. All of us were parish pastors. None of us relished denominational power struggles. Most of the clergy with whom we worked had their primary energies centered in the day-to-day ministry to people in our congregations where it belongs.

In addition to our own organizational limits and general ineptitude as competition for the Preus machine however there was something deeper that held us back. Whether out of training, tradition, instinct, or whatever, all of us had an underlying distaste for exposing the outrages being carried out against faithful brothers and sisters. Public dissent has not been a part of the close-knit brotherhood of ministers and teachers in the denomination in which so many of us have lived side by side since our prep school, college, and Seminary days. Added to this is the strong sense among laity that criticizing the Synodical president is very bad form. The Preus people were able to get away with it so successfully earlier because they claimed from the start that there was false doctrine gaining a foothold in seminary classrooms, teacher training colleges, synodical staff offices, and even overseas missionary posts. Just what false doctrine, and exactly who was allegedly guilty was left aside. But any claim and cry of doctrinal wobbliness was enough to float a mushrooming cloud of suspicion over any and all who did not meet the Preus Party specifications of orthodoxy. The evangelical wing of the Synod, or "moderates" as we were labeled—unhappily in my judgment—cried out against the unChristian treatment given faithful people. Our adversaries cried out that false doctrine was abroad in the Synod. We focused upon people. They fastened upon an abstraction. The later results proved that their approach prevailed, and to this day it puzzles me that so many clergy and so many more laity in the Synod did little or nothing while the most gifted and faithful people in the Missouri Synod were turned out.

Interpreting this whole turn of events to the Grace congregation was not a task that I sat down and theorized about and then designed a master plan to bring it about. My communication to the congregation of my own leadership efforts in the Synod were direct, but hardly frequent and concentrated. I had the assurance that the members trusted my motives and my judgment. I also believed that parishioners do not thrive on one—issue ministry, that issue being an incessant jeremiad about the controversies going on in the denomination at large. A review of my pastoral letters to the members during the early 1970's show infrequent and only passing reference to Synodical problems. The Missouri Synod and its internal agonies were the top religious news story in the American newspaper and magazine world for several years from 1973 on, and I had no doubt that our members read of their Synod and sometimes of their pastor in the Chicago papers and the national news magazines. But it takes a certain mentality that only a handful of members appeared to possess to make the church squabble the main event in all our gatherings as a parish. That mentality spells death for the evangelical spirit of a Christian community. It falls under the Biblical judgment of "stupid controversies, dissensions, and futile quarrels". (Titus 3:9)

In January of 1971 I scheduled the first of some ongoing, informal sessions for members of Grace concerning the embroilment in the Synod at large and my part in it. Out of a parish of some 1750 communicants, the number of those who came was about 35. And among the 35 was a disproportionate number of people who were there not so much to listen as to bring public criticism of my efforts. The tone as well as content of some of their questions that evening gave me some needed education as to where some of our own members were heading. Inquiries about who paid for telephone, postage, and stationery costs were legitimate, but there is a way of asking questions that accuses rather than seeks information. That spirit was not too subtle in the room that evening. Above all, I learned that in the minds of a minority of our members, my efforts along with my clergy colleagues were viewed as the left wing. Such left wing characterization, of course, meant that I had no business criticising the "right wing", since I was falling into precisely the same trap as I was opposing. And in the middle position was placed the Synodical president and those who had come to power with him. It did not occur to me initially, but later I reflected upon the hard fact that some people, at least, were not interested in the fundamental issues and what was happening to people all over the Synod, but were ready to place it all in the framework of left, right, and center political positions. The fact that this happened (with much assistance from the political and social turbulence of the American scene in the late 1960's and early 1970's) so easily is not to be laid to the door of those who phrased it thus. It can be laid at our own door for our failure to make the basic theological point underlying the hue and cry about alleged false doctrine.

In 1971, while so many parishioners and pastors of the Synod were hoping that things would somehow balance out and the life in the denomination would go on as usual, Grace Church received a jolt that few other parishes could feel so directly.

Specific charges of false doctrine were brought against one

of the most respected members of our congregation, Dr. Ralph Gehrke. He served as chairman of the department of religion at Concordia Teachers College, and had taught hundreds of Grace parishioners in Sunday morning adult Biblical studies. He had joined Grace Church in 1962 and quickly became established as our parish Biblical theologian. To speak of him as only a theologian would be to miss some key facets of the man Ralph Gehrke is. His modest, deeply pastoral way with people of all ages and all educational circumstances endeared him to those who had never had formal theological training and would only be put off by overly technical methods of teaching and understanding the Bible. Gehrke taught the Scriptures as one who believes its words as God-given, inspired by the Holy Spirit, authoritative as the only source and norm for faith and life, and the inerrant witness to God's will to bring sinful human beings to the saving knowledge of His truth in Jesus Christ His Son.

But such a faith, so Biblically grounded and essentially Lutheran in its stress upon the Bible as the living Word God speaks to all ages of humankind, was not enough.

A pastor in a nearby suburb of Chicago had been pressing for action against Gehrke since 1962, shortly after Professor Gehrke had come to Concordia Teachers College. Among other things, the point of the charge of false doctrine was that Gehrke refused to affirm that every detail of the Genesis 1-3, Ruth and Jonah was literally factual, nor did he teach the numbering system of the so-called life spans of the patriarchs in the Genesis 5-11 genealogies to be literally factual, nor did he teach that the entire 66 chapters of the Book of Isaiah to be the work of one author. The charges against Gehrke all had to do with a literalist interpretation of the above mentioned passages of the Bible. The line of reasoning went thus: if one does not believe that the snake actually talked, that Noah lived 930 years, that Jonah was in the belly of the great fish for three days, and that the Book of Isaiah has but one author, then what follows is the undercutting of the main message of the Bible that God has created us, redeemed us from sin, and sent His Spirit as the bearer of Christ's kingdom in the world. The truth of the Gospel and the power of God for salvation is made to rest upon human deductions requiring a literalistic interpretation of certain passages in the Old Testament named above. Thus the Gospel is no longer the center of one's view of the entire Bible as the inspired word of God. Rather, man's views about the Bible as being inerrant in all matters of genealogy, numerical statistics, and literalistic interpretation are put at the center of the Bible. Such a notion may be held as one's personal matter of piety, but the Bible itself makes no such claim about itself and such a view is foreign to the confessional Lutheran view of Scripture in its relation to faith.

The popular notion that was promoted by the charges against Gehrke is that he "did not believe the Bible", that he taught that the Bible is full of errors, that he denies the inspiration of the Bible and thus destroys faith.

Such charges were not only incomprehensible to the members of Grace Church who, year after year, had grown in the Word through Dr. Gehrke's instruction, they were deeply offensive. Gehrke, a single man in his fifties, is as close to the Biblical picture of "saint" as most of us come, and charges pressed so relentlessly against him for years took on the appearance of an attack upon the handiwork of God's own Spirit in the life of a gifted, committed Christian man.

Thus Grace congregation had a special opportunity, a particular challenge, to view the allegations of false doctrine broadcast throughout the Synod in the light of accusations centered upon a fellow member within the parish family. Gehrke's colleagues, his President at Concordia, Martin Koehneke, and the Board of Control at Concordia Teachers College in River Forest, Illinois, stated on various occasions that Ralph Gehrke was not guilty of any breach of faith in his calling as a teacher in the church. But these actions in his behalf did not succeed in quieting the charges against him. It was as though one lived in a system where charges are brought back against a person repeatedly, until finally one finds a tribunal that will agree with the charges and convict the person!

Gehrke's work as Biblical study leader at Grace increased as the charges against him continued. He led studies in the resurrection of Christ according to the Gospel writers of the New Testament in the post-Easter Sundays of the spring of 1971. The following autumn he conducted Sunday morning Bible studies for adults on God's Mission to the World, based on the Book of Isaiah. In the winter season he led several Sunday afternoon/evening seminars on how the books of the Bible came down to us in their present form. These were splendid opportunities for members to study not just about the Bible, but to come face to face with the text of Holy Scripture itself and to do so under the guidance of a trusted, sound teacher in the Faith. The Sunday afternoon/evening seminars began at 4 P.M. and continued till the 5:30 break for a fellowship supper, and then continued from 6:30 till 8 P.M. closing. Those were memorable hours, and the core of fifty or sixty parishioners who took part were drawn closer together in the unique fellowship which the Word itself creates.

Most of those who were most willing to believe the accusations against Gehrke were never present for these Bible study hours. That told us something about controversy in the congregation and denomination at large. There is such a thing as the "Do not bother me with the facts—I would rather fight than learn" mentality. Some people can gain notoriety mainly and only through participating in controversy. It's like the story of the Irishman who spotted a fist fight across the street, and immediately crossed over, already rolling up his sleeves and asking, "Is this a private slug fest or can anyone join in?'' There was not much one can do for those whose mind was stubbornly closed against Gehrke. The issue had little to do with methods and meaning of understanding the varied ways in which God speaks to us in Scripture. It had to do with power politics, control over others by the organizational leadership, and continued harassment of those who do not measure up to the party line. This is a deadly evil let loose in the Christian community. To underestimate its presence is to err seriously.

As the next two years progressed, and my pastoral ministry to Ralph Gehrke continued, I saw the heavy toll which continuous accusation of false doctrine takes on a man's spirit. It was one thing for him to have to bear the onus of charges raised by a neighboring pastor. It was another thing to have these charges broadcast nation wide through a newspaper published by the accusing pastor's brother in a small Missouri town southwest of St. Louis. The newspaper, ironically named ''Christian News'' was the most important means the ultra-right wing of the Missouri Synod had to promote their cause, and they did it effectively. The tactic is to repeat cliches and innuendoes loud and long enough until enough people will start believing them and forget that they are allegations instead of proven facts.

The tide against Dr. Gehrke took a new turn with the arrival of Paul Zimmerman as the new president of Concordia Teachers College in the fall of 1973. Zimmerman was known as a strong supporter of the ultra conservative cause and took an active part in the political movement which brought Jacob Preus to the Synodical presidency. He and Preus were faculty colleagues in earlier days at Bethany College in Mankato, Minnesota, a school of the arch conservative wing of the Norwegian Lutherans. President Zimmerman, soon after he had settled into the presidency at River Forest, took the position that all the previous statements of the Concordia administration and Board affirming

Gehrke's soundness as a Lutheran scholar and teacher of the Scriptures were insufficient. Under the rubric of "clearing the matter up conclusively" Zimmerman eventually not only accepted the charges against Gehrke as worthy of pursuit but proceeded to attempt to expand the range of the allegations against his own religion department chairman! Such was the result of repeated personal sessions between Dr. Gehrke and President Zimmerman, with the former attempting to impart to the latter the deepest beliefs of his heart as well as the fruits of a lifetime of Biblical scholarship.

It is the mark of Christ-given dialog when people who disagree on spiritual matters seek to build each other up in the Divine Word rather than to gain points and ultimately prove oneself over the other. The Biblical image of Christians speaking the truth in love, set forth by St. Paul in Ephesians 4, is the picture of people who realize that each belongs to Christ, each has weaknesses and growing to do, each is bent upon helping the other see more and more clearly the glory of Christ in the Scriptures. The purpose of dialog is that Christ might be pre-eminent in all things. But this delicate, finely wrought purpose is put under great jeopardy when one of the participants in the dialog has administrative power over the other. The sessions between President Zimmerman and Professor Gehrke resulted in Gehrke's being required to stand trial as a teacher of false doctrine.

By the time the formal charges of heretical teaching and the trial procedures were underway, Ralph Gehrke was showing the effects of fourteen years of harassment. This strong but gentle-mannered man was becoming increasingly troubled, not only because of the continuing cloud over his entire vocation as a Christian and a called teacher in the church but because of the repeated injustices and failures to let *his own* expressions of insight and belief come through to his overseers. His convictions were constantly being rephrased in summaries Zimmerman was providing the Board, and the *Christian News* misrepresentations of his faith continued to condition many thousands of laity and clergy against him throughout the Synod.

In the midst of these critical circumstances, in a time when Gehrke was harder and harder pressed to maintain his own spiritual balance and emotional equilibrium, the elders of Grace Church invited Dr. Gehrke to present his faith and understanding to the congregation in a formal essay he prepared for the Voter's Assembly in the spring of 1975. Several hundred members packed the Fellowship Hall to listen carefully as our fellow parishioner patiently and carefully covered the specific charges against him with his own response of faith and understanding as a Biblical scholar. It was in one sense outrageous that a man of this stature and fidelity would even have to be invited to speak to the issues raised against him. But in another sense it was a splendid moment for congregation and accused member. It was a powerful learning experience for several hundred of our members, not only to grow in Biblical understanding but also to have revealed to us the demonic things which can happen to Christians *because* they stand so firmly in the Scriptures. Living under the Word, as Martin Luther discovered, is no tranquil venture. It brings a person hardship and disrepute, because the Bible itself is such a profoundly revolutionary Book. It bears witness to God's righteous will to "pluck up and break down, to destroy and overthrow" the principalities and powers which arise against Him in the church as well as world (Jeremiah I), as well as to build and plant and restore. The systematic dismantling of Ralph Gehrke's career in the Missouri Synod as a gifted, faithful teacher of Holy Scripture was a stern lesson for Grace Church members as to what was really ailing the denomination. That *this* man was the kind of person the Synodical machine was finding guilty of false doctrine was a relevation to us, not about Gehrke but about his accusers!

Gehrke's address to the congregation sparked a move by

the parishioners to prepare an appropriate response of affirmation to Dr. Gehrke personally and an appeal to the Synod to recognize him as a man of unquestioned orthodoxy. Some of his faculty colleagues were active in his behalf as well. A group of professors and students contacted over three hundred of Gehrke's former Concordia students who had studied under him in River Forest. The book of testimonial letters was offered to the administration, the Board of Control, and any who wished to read the witness of college students who were in the best position to say what Gehrke believes and what they learned under his guidance.

But the congregational appeal to the Synod and the students' testimony in Gehrke's behalf did not stop the movement to find *one,* at least one live, warm body in whom false doctrine purportedly existed! The denominational commission which eventually judged the case consisted of lay and clergy members who had been elected to their posts with the same manner of political support that had brought Preus to power in 1969. On a June Saturday in 1977, I sat with Ralph Gehrke as his pastor and witness through a day long grilling he received at the hands of his judges. The day, which began at 9 a.m. and ended at 7 p.m. was an exhausting, dismal experience, very distant from the Ephesians 4 spirit of imperfect Christians attempting to build each other up in the stature of Christ. It came as no surprise months later when that panel of judges ruled that Gehrke was guilty of at least four counts of false doctrine as charged nearly 15 years earlier. Basic justice in our secular courts would have paid attention to the repetition of charges against him following affirmation of him by previous college administrations. There would have been attention given to the statute of limitations which mean that in a democracy a citizen need not live out his career with unresolved charges against him remaining like the sword of Damocles. In the spring of 1978 Ralph Gehrke was formally expelled from the Lutheran

Church—Missouri Synod. The district president who performed the final act of the drama, Edmund Happel, avoided the harsh reality of the action by sending him a brief, formal letter with the information that "his name had been removed from the clergy roster". Gehrke refused to carry the matter further on appeal.

Gehrke's effectiveness as a teacher in the Missouri Synod was over, but, as people of faith have learned throughout the ages, as one door closes another is opened. If the people in power at Concordia College and the Missouri Synod were determined to find Ralph Gehrke guilty of false doctrine, there were others ready to recognize his qualities of mind and spirit and put them to work. Pacific Lutheran University, which had already gathered in other talented victims of the Missouri Synod purge, called Dr. Gehrke to join their faculty in Tacoma, Washington, in the spring of 1975. He accepted, and spoke briefly at a Service of Commendation at Grace Church in connection with his leaving Concordia, River Forest, and going to Pacific Lutheran University (a school of the American Lutheran Church).

Gehrke was not alone in his experiences of vocational uprooting. Just over a year previous, 45 out of the fifty faculty of Concordia Seminary, St. Louis, had joined the 450 out of 600 students of the school in a dramatic move into Exile rather than continue under the harassment of the Preus administration. The Jesuits of St. Louis University received these Lutherans and gave them a place to study and learn on their campus for a two year period before more permanent quarters were found in St. Louis. The spring Gehrke left Concordia eight faculty left Concordia Seminary, Springfield, Ill. rather than continue on under conditions which made their teaching impossible. Thirteen members of the eighteen member staff of World Missions of the Synod resigned, and offered their services to the newly formed confessional movement for evangelical Lutheranism that had been formed in 1973. College presidents of Missouri Synod schools were under fire and some chose to resign rather than capitulate. It was an unprecedented denominational shakeup in Lutheran history in the U.S.A., and ranks among the major upheavals in any church body in this country since its founding.

If more congregations would have had the situation we did at Grace, in which the eye of the storm was pinpointed on a parishioner, the larger story of Synodical involvement might have read differently. We cannot stand in judgment of other laity and pastors who seemed so often to sum it all up as a tempest mainly in the St. Louis teapot. Our experience simply told us that "when one member suffers we all suffer". (I Corinthians 12:36) But the Gehrke experience in Grace Church was preparation for other things coming. His departure meant not that we were relieved of a controversial member. We lost a most valued man of Christ from our immediate circle. Furthermore, we were to face sterner tests coming without his physical presence, but very much with his spiritual legacy intact in our midst.

CHAPTER 4

Tightening Pressures on the Parish

While I hope it can be said that I am a person with normal and healthy emotions, I am not given to shedding tears very often.

But several moments came for me during the July, 1973 convention of the Missouri Synod in New Orleans when weeping was the only and the right outlet for the fulness of my feelings over what I saw take place in the space of two weeks of denominational convening.

The occasion was on Thursday, July 12, when a 55% margin of votes by the delegates placed the majority of the faculty of Concordia Seminary, St. Louis, under the judgment of being guilty of teaching false doctrine. The guilty ones were spiritual brothers who put their lifetime vocations of ministry on the line rather than knuckle under to the ultra-right which was taking over the Synod at that convention.

A convention hall, approximately the size of Wrigly Field in Chicago, with over a thousand delegates eligible to speak and vote, is a poor place in which to discuss the more profound aspects of theological understanding. This is not to say that matters of faith and dogma have no place in a denominational setting, but there are different and better ways for men and women of faith to attend to the deepest convictions of the heart.

That vote of condemnation of the faculty which had taught me in my own formative years, the judgment brought down on men of the caliber of Richard Caemmerer, Alfred Fuerbringer, Arthur Carl Piepkorn, Herbert Bouman, Arthur Repp, and several dozen others—many of whom were classmates in my seminary years—cut deeply into my heart.

I thought of Otto Geiseman, and his close kinship in the evangelical spirit of Lutheranism with these men who had just been declared holders of false doctrine. My mind ranged back over a century and more of evangelically minded pastors, professors, and missionaries at home and abroad whose whole lifetimes of rich ministerial service in the evangelical tradition of Lutheranism was also being judged and condemned by the action of 55% of the laity and clergy present in the vast convention hall.

As those of us who were being condemned began singing "The Church's One Foundation Is Jesus Christ Her Lord" my feelings overflowed, and I was not the only person who wept. A similar moment had occured several days earlier when by the same slender majority of 55/45% the delegates had declared the theological statement of President Jacob Preus to be in accord with Scripture in all of its parts and therefore binding on all members of the Synod. That action followed several days of the most intense debate and pleading from delegates that to elevate the Preus "Statement of Scriptural and Confessional Principles" to the status of binding on our faith was to put the knife right into the heart of what it means to be Lutheran in our response to Holy Scripture as the only source and norm for faith and life in the church.

But the arch conservative machine was a powerful juggernaut, not to be sidetracked or stopped at the convention where its adherents were going for broke. In their minds the Missouri Synod had fallen on dangerous times, and the old Missouri was in danger of shipwreck. Their efforts were relentless for years and even several decades earlier. This was their hour.

It was also the hour when I came to the realization that the Preus administration had changed my denominational home with such a violent wrenching from its origins and its own constitution, that I no longer could be at home within it. The action of making Preus's views on the Bible, church mission, and unity with other Christians binding on my own soul was one I could not accept. If there was one cardinal principle in the whole construct of Missouri Synod Lutheran doctrine it was this: binding doctrine is not and cannot ever be determined by majority vote in a Synodical convention. One's inmost conviction of the heart and soul can never be subject to the inevitable political process of a denominational convention. Furthermore, judging faithful brothers to be "no longer tolerated in the church of God" is a shabby business in the midst of parliamentary wrangling and shameless political maneuvering by the party in power at the New Orleans convention. At the time, the meeting appeared to me to be one unrelieved catastrophe, and it was among the most devastating spiritual experiences of my life to see it unfold from day to day.

Two years earlier, at the Synod in Milwaukee, Wisconsin, the groundwork was laid for the New Orleans debacle. At that convention our evangelical forces had appeared to withstand the Preus party charge to make his Statement binding. It was defeated narrowly, and when the vote defeating it was announced a very red-faced and angry Synodical president gave the delegates a severe tongue lashing for failing to put into his hands the tools he regarded as necessary for restoring the Synod to his version of doctrinal health. One delegate, however, had touched the heart of the problem of adding such documents as the Preus version of Christian orthodoxy to the confessional standards of Holy Scriptures, the Apostles, Nicene, and Athanasian Creeds, and the classic documents of the Lutheran Reformation. He likened it to trying to solve a troubled marriage by adding more words to the wedding vow. Nothing is gained by that. In fact the problem is further complicated when one member tries to "win" by simply asserting its will over the other, at the expense of the fundamental covenant which brought the pair together originally. The analogy fits the Missouri Synod. The tragic direction was to no longer stand together under the Scriptures, but to have one party in the Synod say in effect: "I know exactly what the Bible means in all its passages—accept it or get out".

I could not wait to leave the New Orleans convention hall and return to the real world of Grace Church. The lighter moments in the convention had included a marvelous pen and ink drawing presented to Pastor Bert Frey and me by our evangelical colleagues: it pictured the distress of being shafted by a giant tack and was subtitled: "The George McGovern Award For Political Excellence"! Good moments, too, were shared by men and women of spirit and courage who were beginning to recognize that out of the death of the Missouri Synod we had all known there were the faintest beginnings of something new—an evangelical fellowship that did not die because of a denomination convention but lived by virtue of firm roots in the Scriptures and Christ-given love for each other. The New Orleans days had taught me that the effort of mounting a network of dissent from the new ways of power politics in the Synod did not turn out at all in the manner in which we hoped they might. The far right had prevailed in 99% of the offices elected at New Orleans! But winning and losing are words deserving carefuly scrutiny in the language of faith. Losing political victory in the denomination meant being moved, pushed, and oftentimes shoved toward new beginnings in the Spirit which none of us could see with clarity at the time. Besides, it is never loss to see men and women care so deeply about faith and fellowship in the church that they are willing to put themselves, their vocational security, their family comforts, their household and earthly goods on the line rather than play it safe within the denominational womb. That is a false security. It is also a powerful temptation.

Coming home from New Orleans I began wondering how to translate the dynamics of such a two weeks experience to our membership. Fellow parishioner Walter Christopher was a voting delegate, and his wife Maxine was also a personal witness to the fateful sessions. A half dozen other members who were advisory delegates from Concordia College were present as well. These would all prove helpful, but finally there is no way to bring a congregation of 1750 people the full, direct impact of an experience such as this was. It would be futile to try, and a waste of spiritual energy to become overly frustrated because the whole membership at Grace Church could not resonate to the seismic shock waves gripping the convention and promising devastating consequences for the congregations and agencies of the Synod.

I waited a week upon returning before addressing the issue of the convention results in a sermon. The members sensed it was coming. They had read daily news reports in the Chicago papers. The sermon a week following the convention was not the time and place to rehearse the infighting and political machinations of the convention. It was the time and place to proclaim the central article of our Scriptural faith, that man believes with the heart and so is justified before God by the trust of the heart in Christ the Lord. The opposite of that is living under the law of human ordinances and man-centered power in the denomination and/or congregation. What this essential proclamation of the Gospel meant for us at Grace Church at the moment was said thus, in my sermon of July 22, 1973, based upon Romans 10:10: "For man believes with his heart and so is justified, and he confesses with his lips and so is saved".

"I begin this sermon by doing what the text says Christians do, confessing with my lips the faith that is in my heart:

"I believe in the living God, Who brought all things into being from nothing and Who sustains my life and yours to this moment. His miraculous power of creating is evident to me in the birth of my children and yours, and in the countless ways He surrounds me with providential love in daily life. I believe that in all things of life He is at work bringing good out of evil, for He has shown this supremely in the sending of His beloved Son, Jesus Christ our Lord, into our fallen world to rescue me and all mankind from sin. I believe that Jesus is Lord. His birth of the Virgin Mary, His life of ministry and miracles, all come to their fulfillment in His atoning death upon the cross and His glorious resurrection and ascension. I believe the Gospel of God's grace for me in Christ because He has sent the Holy Spirit to dwell in my heart through the Word of forgiveness that is proclaimed in preaching and offered in the Sacraments of Baptism and Communion. I believe that my purpose in life as a pastor, husband, father, and citizen is motivated by Christ's love for me. I gladly affirm the Holy Scriptures of God's written Word to me and to you, and with all Christians throughout the world today and in ages past, I look forward to the resurrection of the body and life eternal with the whole company of heaven.

"This testimony to you from my heart is not the result of the decision of men concerning what is binding on my soul and conscience. This testimony is the handiwork of the Holy Spirit, Who has been at work in my heart through the Word since the time of my baptism 45 years ago. Human decisions and efforts to regulate my faith life cannot penetrate to the deepest reaches of my inner life and spiritual center. That seat of my existence and center of my soul is where God's working, not man's prevails. The text calls this "the heart". Man believes with his heart. Believes what? That God our merciful Father has made us His own beloved children through His Son. With my heart I trust Him—in life and in death. Every believer does. God's mighty works are not only that He is Who He is and does what He does. His mightiest work is that we believe Him with the heart and confess that faith gladly and freely with our lips!

"This heart of mine, which offers you the testimony of faith you have heard, has something else to say to you today. From my heart I tell you that the key decision of our Synod's recent Convention in New Orleans runs head on into the message of this text and the deepest convictions we hold as Lutheran Christians. By a 562-455 vote the delegates declared that President Preus's "Statement of Scriptural and Confessional Principles" be elevated to the status of a doctrinal statement, binding on all members of the Lutheran Church-Missouri Synod.

"From my heart I tell you that is wrong.

"It is right for Synodical Convention delegates to hear matters of doctrinal importance and try to understand them.

"It is right for Synodical Conventional delegates to express themselves concerning their understanding of doctrinal issues.

"It is right for Synodical Convention delegates to make every effort to admonish, reprove, encourage and edify each other with the clear teachings of Holy Scripture.

"But it is wrong for Synodical Convention delegates to assume that a majority vote makes a resolution on doctrine binding on the conscience of anybody.

"That is wrong—disastrously wrong!

"It is wrong because God's Word alone, not man's, can bind the conscience, soul, and heart of the Christian.

"That is what Martin Luther's reforming work is all about. Popes and councils can err, he said. It is the Word alone that can bring conviction, obedience of faith, and joyful, free confession of that faith from the heart.

"It is wrong because the action of making convention resolutions on doctrine binding sets us on the path to sectarianism ("we alone have the true measure of what is Scriptural") and off the path of Lutheranism as a confessional movement in the mainstream of Christianity.

"It is wrong because it flies directly in the face of our own Synodical tradition. Our Constitution states so clearly: "All matters of doctrine and of conscience shall be decided only by the Word of God. All other matters shall be decided by a majority vote''. (Article VIII C)

''It is wrong because it rejects the conviction and insight of our most honored spiritual fathers in the Missouri Synod. Franz Pieper stated it with unmistakable clarity:

> 'Christ has commissioned neither some one person (Pope, princes, governors, presidents, etc.) nor a college of persons (bishops, pastors, boards of directors, consistories, parliaments, conferences, synods, councils, etc.) to decide and ordain ecclesiastical matters for the Church in any way binding the conscience. . . . In general, when the power to make binding decisions and laws in the Church is said to inhere in any body of men, be they ecclesiastics or laymen or a mixed board, this is not a Christian but a Papistic position, because in the Christian Church God's Word is the only authority and all Christians are and remain responsible directly to God for all they believe and do. . . .'

''I understand the anguish others feel over the divided Synod in which we walk together as brothers and sisters in faith. I feel that, too. I can understand the impulse to settle things for good with Convention resolutions. Those resolutions deserve our utmost seriousness and attention, but they remain under the Word. And we remain under the Word. The way to solve our difficulties is not talking about the Word but getting into it together and staying under the power of the Gospel till we agree! We must hear it together. We must do it together. And that hearing and doing can bring blessing only as it takes place in Christ-like love and mutual trust.''

What it meant for us in the longer range we would be learning, step by step and month by month.

The plunge into the usual September flurry of parish

activity in 1973 was healthy for me and for all of us. Ministering to people in all the joys and problems of life helped me heal over from the shellshock of the July days in New Orleans. I have often compared the resources of ministry in the parish with other types of Synodical office and staff ministries when it comes to finding and keeping balance in one's mind and soul. I respect my colleagues who are called to a particular function on a denominational staff and benefit along with everyone else from their labors. But when controversy closes in on a denomination with the force and intensity of that which descended upon the Missouri Synod, I had extra reason to be grateful for the parish base of my own calling. I learned that when my mail or telephone would bring me some particularly distressing news of yet one more brother subjected to accusation and obstruction in his work, my own chagrin and gloom over such things would be lifted by going to work with people in the tasks immediately at hand. People who are seriously ill or gratefully recovered, youth who are wrestling with themselves or their parents, people who are giving their best as Christians on the job and are taking sharp reactions in stride, teaching children the Scriptures, ministering the Word of eternal life to aged men and women—holding forth that renewing Word to those still outside the faith—these are the things that would draw me out of the doldrums again and again.

At the heart of my ministry to others to keep me from despairing over Synodical problems was their ministry to me, beginning especially with my wife and family. It is marvelously bracing to be able to come home with frustrations and anxieties in my mind, and share them with my wife, Beverly. Her capacity to listen is a great gift, as every person in the clergy knows who is blessed with such a spouse. Our four children, though not yet old enough to grasp what it was all about, kept on cheering me and helping me realize that if God be for us who can be against us! As a family we tried not to make the gory details of congregation and Synodical difficulties a part of our dinner time conversation. I am dead set against adverse mention of people's names, within or beyond Grace Church in our household. Somewhere, I think from Luther's writings, I learned that admonition not to complain publicly about hard-to-love parishioners but to keep all that within the confines of my daily prayers to God. All this notwithstanding, our youngest son, Joel, would from time to time come into the family conversation from straight out of the blue with questions like, "Dad, is the Synod winning?" Those questions always brought a smile to my face, and helped me to laugh at myself and with others. More than I realized, our children were taking in the events as they slowly gained momentum. I know some preacher's sons and daughters who will carry to their graves spiritual scars inflicted upon them by injudicious spilling over of pastoral hurts upon the children of the parsonage. I do not want to have that happen in our own family.

Along the mainstream of congregation worship, service, and mission, I felt the need was essential for our members to get a closer look at the size of problems that were afflicting the denomination and would surely affect our congregation sooner or later. The elders and Church Council agreed that the best way to start was to have a good look at the Preus *Statement* itself. In early September I invited all Grace members who were interested to attend a serious of eight Sunday morning sessions of an hour each on the document.

I was astounded at the response.

Between 250 and 300 people filled our Fellowship Hall for those Sundays in September and October during the hour between our two morning Services of worship. I wished that as many would flock to a study *of* the Bible, not just *about* it.

I led the study sessions, and was as careful as I could be to point out strengths as well as failures in the document. But my word was hardly the last one or the only one on the materials presented. Debate and discussion was lively and, in the main, positive.

But it was evident from the first ten minutes of the entire series that this document did not unite Christians. It divided us. All one had to do was read its sentences, and the instant response was controversy. Another strong impression that came with the study series was how isolated from actual Christian life today the theses of the document were. The best theology is written in direct partnership with the real world of real people facing real life issues with real faith. The church has had to bear the burden of isolated, overly-academic, non-people related theological discourse throughout all her centuries, but such theological work never really serves because it is not preachable nor do its themes ever become part of the hymnody and the musical heritage of the church. I cannot envision how people will ever gather on Sunday mornings and sing verses of spirited praise about a human notion of Biblical inerrancy. People of the faith can and do praise God for His Word which is lamp for our feet and light upon our path. But the final test of theological expression is whether it is preachable and makes the heart sing. If it's not, it will not edify and misses the mark.

We did more than get a two month look at the Preus *Statement*. We discovered the lineaments of several sides forming up within the congregation. The Sunday morning series did not create them so much as reveal them. The disconcerting thing, however, was that some few of our members were beginning to slip into a dangerous trap—that of maintaining the rightness of the Synod's action on the Preus *Statement* in spite of its contents and the manner in which it had come to occupy the position it did. President Preus himself had offered it several years earlier as "advice" to the Board of Control of Concordia Seminary, whose faculty was under fire from the President and those who shared his point of view. But then, by a curious process of osmosis, it was proposed by the Preus party as a definitive statement of Missouri Synod doctrinal soundness, and was so declared at the 1973 Convention. The document was causing a Synod-wide pro and con movement; we saw the same thing in Grace Church.

Before the concluding session of the Sunday morning series was over, I gave the members a copy of my four page statement of protest against the Preus *Statement* which I sent to the officials of the Synod. The effort was my attempt to put the larger and deeper Scriptural message alongside one man's effort to delineate for a troubled church body what he thought was fully Scriptural. I do not impugn his motives for the effort. But I did take issue with its contents, and above all, with the status given the document as binding on the souls of all of us in the Synod.

I received a mimeographed letter from the Synodical headquarters in St. Louis acknowledging the receipt of my protest—and nothing more. In later months I recall reading Dr. Preus's comment on how relatively few protest statements were sent in. I fail to see the significance of counting the numbers of protest statements and drawing conclusions from such statistics. I was more interested in Synodical response to carefully offered protest statements instead of mimeographed letters saying the letters had arrived. But no such response has ever come.

Instead the Synodical president appointed two groups of ten persons to "delinate the issues and come with a uniform response for peace in the Synod". Ten persons were pro-Statement and ten were against. Clergy and laity were part of each panel, including our member Walter Christopher as a lay participant among the ten taking issue with the Preus *Statement*. Here was one more strange, if not outrageous development. The Preus party labored mightily to pass the *Statement* in Convention as binding, and the Concordia Seminary faculty majority of 46 men was judged to hold to false doctrine that is not to be tolerated in the church of God. Then the President asks twenty people to delineate the issues! The effort appeared to me from the outset as a dodging of serious, Synod-wide probing of what was happening among us. And the requirement that the two sides could not present their delineation of issues, agree on what the issues were and the words in which the issues should be phrased seemed to me as insurance that the group of twenty people never report. As the sessions wore on in St. Louis, each time taking a day out of Mr. Christopher's time as a practicing attorney in a very busy law career, he shared with me the sadness of the whole venture. Key people on the Preus side simply did not take the time to attend the sessions. The final report document appeared three years later, and simply announced the obvious—that agreement on issues was not possible. Meanwhile, the horse was long out the barn door in Synod.

The impact of the Synodical controversy upon the congregation took an interesting turn earlier in 1973, in connection with our Voter's Assembly meetings. Voter's Assemblies at Grace Church had traditionally been low key, and if 30 people attended it was a larger than usual turnout. In the early Geiseman years too many such meetings were occasions for verbal shootouts for those who had nowhere else to dump their frustrations with life in general. Geiseman had once mentioned to me his hunch about inexplainably contankerous people in the congregation. Always look behind and beyond the orneriness of their words, he advised, for something else in their job or marriage or family that was giving them no end of trouble. People will dump their emotional garbage in a congregational meeting because of an instinct that in the church they can let it all come out without damaging retaliation for their outburst. That can't be done in a touchy job situation, or in an already troubled marriage. That bit of advice is part of the reason why he deliberately played down the monthly meeting of voting members of the congregation from his early years of sad experience with church meetings which gave everyone ulcers.

In the late winter of 1973 the word went out that the congregations were to nominate candidates for the Synodical presidential office. Our Church Council had formed a committee to solicit names of nominees from Grace members. My own hope that Grace would nominate the one man I believed to be electable over Jacob Preus. Oswald Hoffman was respected by all sides within the Synod, and was a proven churchman of national stature. His Lutheran Hour preaching Sunday after Sunday made his name a household word amoung Missouri clergy and laity, and his evangelical spirit made him a candidate many of us hoped would return the Synod to its previous way. He fit the Synodical tradition of electing a man who bent over backwards avoiding the appearance of being hungry for the job.

At the March meeting of the Voter's Assembly, there was almost the same several dozen people present to hear the recommendation of the nominating committee and get on with the matter of voting for the nominee from Grace Lutheran Church, River Forest, Illinois. A number of members had done just the lightest touch of pre-meeting telephoning, urging several more of their pro-Preus member friends to attend and join the assembly of that evening. It worked. By a 14-13 margin, our parish nominated Jacob Preus for the presidency. It was hardly the ecclesiastical event of the decade. Although I was disappointed that we had not sent the name of Oswald Hoffman in as our choice I went to bed convinced that the Kingdom of God was still intact. The next morning, however, my telephone began to ring in my office and for the next several days religious editors from daily newspapers from Chicago, Milwaukee, Minneapolis, St. Louis and Los Angeles were wanting to talk with me about how it happened that the "Lueking" parish backed Jack Preus.

I have always disapproved of the careless talk whereby any congregation of Christians is called by the name of its pastor. It is Grace Church, not Lueking Church. Having made that point I went on to inquire how the word of doings in our small corner of the Vineyard had gotten to religious editors who certainly must have more substantial news to report to their readers than this. Religion editors, whom I have most often liked and respected, were being professional, I suppose, in guarding their sources. Be it as it may, it was again evident that a number of our own members were eager to get this report out instantly. This was a situation that was not to end with that third Tuesday in March, 1973. I was to learn that it would continue and increase over the years ahead. There was nothing to do except confirm the story, make sure they had the count right (14-13, in a parish of well over a thousand potential voters), and then inquire if they would be interested in some more important things I thought Grace was all about! No doubt if the vote had been 14-13 the other way and I would have been called about a Hoffman nomination, I would have been more kindly to the news stories which followed! The following Sunday, our Bach Cantata homilist at Grace happened to be Oswald Hoffman. He had read about the vote in the St. Louis papers, and thought the entire thing should be treated with a loud guffaw than gnashing of teeth. I found his advice refreshing and was glad to take it. Subsequent gloating in the right-wing publications of the Synod was forthcoming as sure as the sunrise, and I answered the kind brothers who wrote me letters of consolation with the Hoffmanesque touch of humor.

One lasting result did occur within Grace Church, however, and this was one which our right wing friends within and beyond the congregation did not consider. From that time on, no voter's assembly at Grace Church was attended by less than one hundred people and many of them exceeded an attendance of three hundred! From that time on, the voting membership carried on unbroken series of crucial decisions which in every case leaned toward the evangelical direction. Looking back on that quirky evening in March, 1973, I am grateful we got a shaking up when we needed it—at the beginning of the long journey we were to make as a congregation through some tight turns and narrow passages. The month after month (with summer respite) schedule of voter's meetings have often seemed more to be anticipated with a sigh than a Hallelujah. Many suggestions have come along that we should do away with that schedule and settle for one town meeting-type assembly of the whole congregation per year. But the long way around of participatory democracy, as the saying puts it nowadays—has proven far more beneficial than detrimental. People need a time and a place, consistently offered, in which questions can be asked, points pursued, information mulled over, and issues debated. After all, Grace congregation was objecting strongly to high-handed power politics, and it would hardly do for us to take away ground from our own argument by removing the opportunity for everyone to come and have his say.

As the months and seasons of congregational involvement continued, with things so often coming up for crucial decision in the voter's assemblies, I learned something new about my own experience as pastor of Grace Church. Along about Monday afternoon before the Tuesday evening voter's assemblies each month, I would begin to sense a cloud of apprehension settling in on my spirit. I suppose my family could detect an edge in my voice as my patience would wear thin over inconsequential matters at home. The temptation would be there *not* to trust the Gospel, nor the Holy Spirit, nor the solid, dependable, evangelically-minded people of Grace Church to keep on rising to each occasion. That temptation, present in my soul in the subtle feelings of what the Germans call *Anfechtung* (a gloomy spirit of anxiety when put to the test) did not come at me in any other aspects of my ministry. Even in the face of what is the most demanding circumstance of pastoral ministry, the burial of a child and ministry to the grieving family, I did not experience this feeling. It was, and sometimes still is, my most palpable brush with the demonic. It shows me my own mortal self, still in need of grace and mercy from the Lord Christ. It is humbling, yet instructive.

This experience helps me understand something more of the mystery of God's permitting hard things to happen and keep on happening in our lives. I can understand from this minor dose of pre-meeting agitation of spirit some small part of the much larger soul struggles that other people of the Faith, past and present, have endured. It provides me with my own assignment of dealing with that part of Christian life which Karl Rahner calls "a wintry sort of spirituality". More popularized offerings of the Christian life which promise only blue sky brightness and uninterrupted smoothness of discipleship are not true to Christ's own word for us "In this world you shall have tribulation, but be of good cheer, I have overcome the world" (John 16:33).

This is as good a place as any to add another insight which has become a permanent part of my own spirituality as a result of traveling this journey of obedience in faith with the congregation I love and serve. While none of us seeks controversy for its own sake, and none of us enjoys it, we nevertheless are called to face it and to understand that *this* is the context that is given us for our life and work together as Grace Church. It is not the permanent setting, for these circumstances will not last forever. But it is the present setting that is given us. We did not choose the situation in which we were called to show forth the light of Him Who calls us from darkness to light. To be sure, we were called to be peacemakers, and there was already abundant contentiousness in the world without Christians adding to it. But were we exempt from the deep and mysterious pressures and anxieties of existence which visit all humans in some form or another? And could we assume that we lived in an airy aloofness from spiritual adversaries such as those which caused Paul the Apostle to bare his own soul in these words:

> "We are afflicted in every way, but not crushed; perplexed but not driven to despair; persecuted but not forsaken; struck down but not destroyed." (II Cor. 4:8-9)

Living the Gospel as a Christian community is always more demanding than living under the Law, and the collected customs and usages of human origin which can move into determinative importance with fatal ease in a congregation. Yet the former is Life-giving; the latter is the dead hand of legalism upon the people and will ultimately quench the Spirit.

Therefore, I should add that the vexations, interruptions, outrages and unexpected difficulties of charting the congregation direction according to the free course of the Gospel all served to accentuate the Gospel as the true treasure and only lasting foundation of congregation life. And all the things which accentuate the Gospel, including the anxious, gloomy moments, were to be counted as all joy—because they served to make one point clear: the Gospel is everything and there is no other power that brings us to God our Father and holds us to Him with a steadfast, happy heart!

Whenever kind people have offered their condolences for what we were called upon the undergo at Grace, I want to somehow get these thoughts across. It isn't always possible, but the desire is there nonetheless.

The rising level of congregation awareness that we were a bellweather congregation brought us an experience that had a quite different effect than what was intended. Anonymous letters had been sent to the pastor in earlier years. (Geiseman would sometimes get them on Christmas Eve, a half hour before the Children's Service—and he never opened them till after all the congregation and family celebrating was over!) But mailing to the majority of families of the congregation, taking issue with my ministry in particular or with parish decisions in general, were new. Not all were anonymous. Some were signed by one or several members, who since the year 1971 were most upset over what we were doing and how we were doing it. At first these parish-wide mailings would simply annoy me. I was particularly distressed over the effect they had upon older, shut-in members of Grace Church who could be upset for days on end by a letter in their box raking me over the coals or alleging that Grace—their own congregation—was doing something wrong in the sight of God as well as the Synodical leadership. Time after time, on my communion calls to elderly people, I would have to spend half my time calming people down and explaining that we were not making shipwreck of the Faith. The most common reaction to these letters was anger toward the senders, and it did seem appropriate to me that people who had enough else on their minds did not need several people in Grace Church lecturing them on the dangers of having a pastor and parish mislead them with deception and tricks. But how to put a stop to it? If we passed a voter's assembly resolution, with threats of discipline and expulsion of those who sent out unauthorized mailings, we were muzzling a free expression of opinion in the parish. If we said or did nothing about it, we made faithful people wonder if any member can do anything and get away with it at Grace Church. No little struggle went on in our midst as to how best to deal with the problem, with the decision being never to put people out because they told others of their disagreement. The elders expressed their appeal to all members to use the Voter's Assembly as the proper forum for making their opinions known. I reiterated the same sentiment several times in pastoral letters to all members.

But it did not stop the mailings.

Yet the mailings themselves, often timed to arrive in the mailboxes of the members a day or two before some matter of importance in our relation to the Synod, had the opposite effect than the one apparently intended. People would read a letter haranguing the pastoral and general parish leadership, and lay aside other plans which would have prevented their attending a voter's assembly. Others would be reminded to come, having read the regular notice but then forgetting it. The strength of the whole congregation was being galvanized by these mailings, which so often demonstrated the legalistic, accusatory spirit abroad in the Synod at large in a manner far more effectively than I could have described it.

The irony turned out to be this: without the disturbing, abrasive minority which calls for a loyalty to the present Synodical administration at all costs, the congregation would not have directly confronted the seriousness of the legalism besetting the Synod and thus withdrawn from it. The built-in presence of a group which constantly appealed to human authority and man-made laws, kept on showing us the consequences of setting aside the Scriptural word of forgiveness and the primacy of love, joy, patience, humor, hope, a forgiving spirit, and an open mind.

CHAPTER 5

Keeping the Parish in Context

The series of assistant pastors who have served Grace Church over the years since the late 1940's has added much to the life of the congregation and each has been uniquely blessed in his opportunity to serve here. James Manz has worked faithfully in a fascinating downtown Chicago parish for three decades. Kenneth Breimeier has served as seminary dean and faculty member at Concordia Seminary and Seminex in St. Louis, and continues to use his conseling skills in a specialized clinical pastoral care ministry in that city. Martin Marty is the best known of the assistants at Grace. His two years of service from 1952-1954 helped prepare him for a subsequent career as a churchman whose critique of contemporary religion has made him known internationally as a historian, theologian, and Distinguished Service professor at the University of Chicago, a prolific author and peripatetic speaker throughout the nation. Richard Gotsch serves an active congregation on the northern rim of Chicago and applies his Biblical expertise and pastoral care to people within and beyond the congregation. Paul Firnhaber, though not now in the active pastoral ministry, has continued to make an impact on the world of Christian art and writing—a talent he displayed during his years at Grace in the mid-1960's. Stanley Bahn is now in Appleton, Wisconsin, continuing his steady, modest, faithful way with people of all ages and interests as their pastor. Phillip Bruening serves a congregation in Richmond, Virginia, carrying on those qualities of dedicated ministry which he learned from his late father and which he put into practice at Grace during the tumult of the late 1960's. Ronald Rentner is serving a congregation in the bay area of San Francisco: his support comes from his skills as an investment banker. He is a modern version of St. Pauls's model of self-support in ministry. Frank Janzow brought to the congregation unusual sensitivities in counseling and youth work, skills which he is putting to good use in his present ministry on the outskirts of Milwaukee. A major question came before the congregation in the spring of 1976, when the three year tenure of Pastor Janzow was nearing completion. He was very well liked by all of us in the congregation, and rightly so for his gifts for ministry are abundant. He graduated from Concordia Seminary in 1973, the last class to finish in St. Louis before the storm broke over the seminary in the latter half of the year. The January, 1974, formation of Concordia Seminary in Exile had received international coverage (I recall sitting in the living room of a Lutheran minister in a small East German town in the summer of 1976 and answering his questions about "Seminex" as it was called). When 450 out of 600 students and 55 out of 60 faculty refused to relinquish their theological confession of what sound Lutheranism called for in the face of denominational tyranny, they left the campus of Concordia Seminary, and continued their education in the makeshift arrangements provided by the Jesuits of St. Louis University! Nothing like it had occurred before in American church history; indeed it is difficult to find precedent in western church history for a community of theological students and faculty of this size and prestige to risk all their denominational security for the sake of the belief they held so strongly.

Concordia Seminary in Exile—"Seminex"—graduates were trained entirely within the Missouri Synod system until the final four months of their eight year preparation for ordination. The Preus administration had fought with every strategy imaginable to prevent Seminex graduates from entering the pastorates of Missouri Synod congregation—for obvious reasons. These young men were determined enough in their opposition to the Preus program for the Synod that they laid everything on the line. It is not difficult to understand why the Synodical president did not want them leading congregations.

But the Missouri Synod is *congregational* in its policy, not hierarchical. That is, the denomination does not have the authority to ordain its candidates and send them wherever it chooses. The congregation has authority to ordain, and the congregation calls the candidates to service as pastors.

The implications for these basic themes of faith began to be clarified for Grace Church members in March of 1976. I had begun to discuss the matter of a new assistant pastor with leaders in the congregation and did not have to belabor the point that our next call would be anything but routine. Their perception of the matter was varied, as expected, because each quickly grasped the key point: the way we handled the issue of calling the next assistant pastor was indicative of the way the congregation would move in the crucial months following. Let me sketch a brief profile of three parishioners who represented different shades of understanding and outlook. Wayne Schroeder was a prince of a man. He came from strong Christian training from his day of birth in downstate Illinois. Wayne had been an All-American choice as a football player at Depauw University in Indiana, then had come to Chicago for a splendid career in management with a large paint firm. With his wife, Mildred, he had come to Grace in 1930, and had served in every capacity imaginable. He loved God with an exuberant spirit, and when Wayne sang hymns from his regular place toward the back of the sanctuary, I could hear his strong voice in the chancel! Wayne embodied the best meaning of the word conservative. He cared deeply about conserving the Word of Christ, and the best Lutheran traditions surrounding the Gospel. Wayne had a way of giving himself and the best of his efforts to whatever he was doing, and was especially opposed to dissension within the ranks of the faithful. In his work as sales manager, he saw the problems of splitting the ranks instead of working together under management, and I can recall conversations with him about the headaches he had with work problems. Wayne Schroeder stood for a thoroughly Gospel-centered Lutheranism, and was especially anxious that nothing obstruct the course of that saving Word of Christ laid like seed in young hearts at the elementary and high school level. He had been among the founders of a nearby Lutheran high school in 1955. He had given hours upon hours as one of the best teachers of youth Grace Church has ever had. Although he recognized problems in the Synod instantly, he remained convinced that bucking city hall would bring more grief to the parish than ever it was worth. He quietly accepted the actions of Grace Church in supporting members such as Ralph Gehrke, and he never denied me the privilege of following my own conscience in speaking out against the trends in the denomination since 1970. I did not want Wayne to be denied the freedom of his own convictions as we wrestled with the question of whom to call as my assistant, a Seminex graduate or candidate approved by the Synod. It was agony for him to take a position different from my own, even as it was difficult for him to see the congregation approach a decision which would put it on a collision course with the Preus administration.

Another member, George Reinhardt, is another exemplary layman whose roots were similar to Wayne Schroeder's. He was born downstate in Illinois, had studied medicine at Washington University in St. Louis, received his degree, continued in special residency training in surgery, married a nurse, Judith Lightner, and served overseas as a medical officer in Vietnam. George was the youngest man ever to be elected elder at Grace, and began his three year term of service with little awareness that upon his shoulders would fall the full weight of lay leadership in the congregation's decision to leave the Synod.

George majored in chemistry in college, was instinctively interested in what things are made of, how parts of cells and molecules fit together, etc. His training developed his natural gifts of thoroughness of mind, patient probing of all the available facts, weighing carefully both their content intrinsically and their impact on their environment, and then coming to a decision. If that decision required the courage of moving out beyond the tried and accepted, so be it. Scientific progress occurs that way, and so does progress in every other aspect of life—including that which has to do with applying the unchanging Gospel to new circumstances of the congregation. He was blessed with the capacity to listen, respectfully and carefully, to viewpoints counter to his own. Being twenty years Wayne Schroeder's junior meant that George Reinhardt experienced certain events of the 1960's in a different way. He was in Vietnam himself, and saw day after day the death and bloody suffering of war inflicted upon young American servicemen and Vietnamese civilians of all ages. He was pitched headlong into the center of America's most disastrous political decision—to intervene militarily in southeast Asia, and saw the tragedy resulting from the nation's leadership making policy which was wrong morally, militarily, politically. That gave Dr. Reinhardt a perspective which comes only from personal experience, that the system can be wrong and that the institution must be opposed. This part of his life, coupled with the exemplary spiritual training he received as a youth in his family and now practiced in his own household, and blended with his medical training to examine the facts scrupulously with an openess toward new conclusions, made him better qualified for elder-level leadership than any of us dreamed!

Still another member who reflects another segment of the congregation is Edward Erickson, a Lutheran from his earliest days and blessed with exceptionally strong spiritual roots from his parents and family. Unlike the other two elders, Edward had grown up in another branch of the Lutheran family, the American Lutheran Church. He and his wife, Phyllis, had joined Grace congregation in the 1960's. Within a year of affiliating, he had become active as a Sunday School teacher and gave our fifth grade youth religious instruction second to none. Later, he had been appointed as superintendent of the Sunday School, and gave that major responsibility his best energies and talents. Ed's work was an insurance adjustor, traveling to places destroyed by fire and estimating damages, a line of work that helps a man appreciate anything that stands up and lasts under the force of destruction. By instinct, he, too, abhorred church dissension. He fulfills the apostolic injunction to seek congregational leadership among those who are irenic, stable, able to guide their own households well, and not given to endless arguments and futile disputes. (I Timothy 2:8)

The unique perspective Edward brought as an elder was experience outside the Missouri Lutheran fold. He was not burdened with the parochialism that can beset those who begin sentences in church meetings with "I am a fifth generation Missouri Lutheran"—as though that endowed a man with wisdom and sanctity! His candor about his background, mixed with his sense of humor about the foibles of church folk, made the Synodical controversy both bewildering and extremely distasteful to him. He knew from experience that Christian life can and does flourish in congregations outside the Missouri Synod! His peacableness of disposition however is not to be confused with weakness. If constant internal dissension would so distract and encumber the congregation, he would arrive first among the elders at the conclusion that withdrawal was essential to our life and mission.

The three elders mirrored the outlook of 98% of the

congregation. What they did not reflect was the hardline sentiment of accusing, disrupting, and endlessly engaging in church dispute. In the spring of 1976, as we went to work on the question of calling a new assistant pastor, I could not have been more blessed than to work with these three men. Each had a vital insight to offer, a needed role to exercise.

Added to this was the leaven of Pastor Frank Janzow's own decision to move on after his three years at Grace instead of staying a fourth year. All of us would have been delighted to have had him do so, for the quality of his professional work was of such an order that a fourth year with us would have added depth and breadth to the already impressive swath he had cut in his time with us from his arrival in the summer of 1973. Furthermore, he had completed nearly all but not everything in his graduate program in the field of psychology and counseling. But Frank's mind was made up to seek another call. He took the floor in the April meeting of the Voter's Assembly and said—clearly, firmly, and with love—that his heart was with the brothers at Seminex. If he stayed, a candidate for ministry from Seminex would not have had the opportunity for service at Grace—if that was the decision of the congregation. He then encouraged the congregation to call a new assistant from the ranks of Seminex graduates, thanked parishioners for their kindness in urging him to stay on, but wisely advised us that this decision could not be dodged or postponed for a year. It had to be faced, and now was as good as later!

A son of Grace Church was ready for ordination in June of 1976 as a graduate of Concordia Seminary in Exile. Aaron Sorrels had come with his parents and sisters to Grace Church when he was a first grader, and I remembered him as a bright lad with a ready smile. He had moved to the Pacific Northwest after Grace school graduation, and then had come into the Missouri Synod system of preparation for the ministry that put him in touch with men of excellent theological gifts as teachers of preachers-to-be. During his vicarage year on Long Island, New York, the Seminex community had formed. He and his wife, Deno, came back to St. Louis clear about the Seminex location for his final year of study and graduation. He was also clear about the difficulties this posed for placement. But here he was, and here we were.

The congregation called and ordained Aaron Sorrels, but not without due preparation and full consideration of the consequences. The months of preparations forced us back to Scripture, the Lutheran Confessions, and reflection upon our relationship to the Missouri Synod. This had begun in a related study months before our calling of an assistant pastor. In the late fall of 1975 we had opened up the discussion of transferring our District affliation from the Northern Illinois to the English District. The latter had embodied the evangelical spirit within the church body for over fifty years, and represented a welcome change from the plodding conformity to the Synodical legalism found throughout the Northern Illinois District leadership. The Church Council had invited the presidents of both districts to come to Grace for a discussion with our Council on a series of questions centering around the relationship of Synod and congregation. Harold Hecht, the English District president had come just before Christmas, and Edmund Happel came several weeks later. A summary of their presentations show the striking differences, not just between two district presidents but between two ways of viewing the church in the light of the Gospel. (See Appendix A, p. 171.)

To the surprise of some, the Church Council recommended Grace not transfer to the English District. That recommendation was accepted by the members. The thought in the minds of many of us was that the English District as such was not going to survive very long in the Missouri Synod, and to transfer to a District ticketed for oblivion was not very useful.

The value of the six months of study and discussion was that it kept the focus on the key issue, the central place of the Gospel in the ordering of the church's life and ministry. More than we knew at the time, thethought, Biblical study, and prayer given to the subject of District membership was to serve us as we came to the matter of calling an assistant pastor.

Our approach to the matter represented our effort to be faithful to our evangelical convictions and also responsible in our relation to the Missouri Synod. We voted, overwhelmingly, to call Aaron Sorrels as our assistant. We included the provision that our District President, Edmund Happel, was welcome to come into our midst and bring whomever he wished for the purpose of learning the soundness in faith and the readiness for ministry of the Seminex graduate we called. The Synod had resolved in its previous convention that Seminex graduates must pass a colloquy before being declared ready for call and ordination by a congregation. Our view was that this proposal made no sense. How could a panel of three members determine in several hours time the readiness of a man for the office of the holy ministry? We regarded the faculty of the seminary which trained him over four years time the proper body to declare a man ready to serve a congregation as an ordained pastor. Furthermore, the panel of three comprising the Missouri Synod Colloquy Board were radically and publicly opposed to Seminex. It was like asking George Wallace, Richard Russel, and Herman Talmadge to pass on the fitness of Martin Luther King, Jr. for readiness to serve the country.

The elders and I thought the effort should be made, however, to join Aaron in a conference with the Missouri Synod Colloquy Board on the issues surrounding the entire problem. We went to St. Louis on June 8, the day set for our Voter's Meeting at 8 p.m. It was an instructive experience. Sitting across the table in the Synodical headquarters from the leaders of the church body, Aaron responded courteously to the questions of Synodical Vice President Edwin Weber as to why he was reluctant to go through a formal colloquy. He stated, correctly, that the colloquy was established for ministerial candidates coming to the Synod from outside its doctrine and confession. Sorrels related his lifelong membership within the Synod, and his years of learning at the feet of Synodical mentors in Synodical schools. He had his Biblical and Confessional homework done, and after six hours of polite conversation, we parted company from the Synodical leaders and caught a late afternoon plane for Chicago. We arrived in time for an 8 p.m. meeting, and were greeted by over two hundred parishioners who filled Fellowship Hall to the doors. All were interested in our experience of the day. We told our story, reiterated our convictions, and asked for the support of the men and women of Grace Church.

The debate was spirited, but not acriminious. Wayne Schroeder made a strong appeal to the assembly that we hold off calling Mr. Sorrels until after he had decided to take the colloquy. George Reinhardt expressed his conviction that Aaron Sorrels was ready for ministry, and that the congregation had exercised its Biblical responsibility in calling him at a previous meeting. That sentiment prevailed by a decisive affirmation of the congregation members present.

Following the meeting, which lasted till well past the usual ten o'clock closing hour, I went to my office and phoned the Sorrels in St. Louis. They were elated. We were happy, too. As I finally got to bed, I left the activities of the day in the hands of the Lord of the church—where they always are straightened out and blessed anyway!

Decisive action brings strong counter-action. The Tuesday evening vote to ordain Aaron was followed by his ordination on the Sunday thereafter. But during the intervening days a minority of five members asked to meet with the District President on Saturday. Among their questions to him was their proposal of a court injunction banning or at least postponing the ordination. President Happel, to the credit of his good judgment and his awareness that Lutheran polity places the authority for ordination squarely with the congregation, told them not to proceed with such an idea. This information came to me on Saturday afternoon before the Sunday ordination from George Reinhardt, whom they had invited to accompany them on their morning visit to the Happel residence. Learning of that did not altogether surprise me, nor did it add any joy to the Ordination Service plans the next day. But it did provide a lesson in the atmosphere in which Pastor Sorrels would carry out his two year time of pastoral service with us. There would be a half dozen people of the congregation who would go out of their way to spurn his ministry, regard his ordination as invalid and illegal, and never address him as Pastor Sorrels, always Mister Sorrels. Neither he nor I nor the rest of the congregation pin our faith on whether the clergy is addressed Pastor or Mister. But the truly serious matter was the ostentatious gesture of refusing to commune from the side of the chancel Pastor Sorrels was serving, and publicly questioning whether he was fit to teach children in the parish confirmation classes. These offensive assertions were mild, however, to the questions Synodical President Jacob Preus was asking publicly. In a Florida pastoral conference in which he was opposing the placement of Seminex graduates, he inquired whether husbands would want graduates of an "illegal seminary" making pastoral calls in the homes of parishioners where the wife was at home alone during the day.

The Ordination Service on Sunday morning, June 13, 1976, was among the most meaningful in which I have ever participated. The visiting clergy who accepted our invitation to join in the traditional laying on of hands and speaking Scriptural passages of blessing were each aware of the consequence of being present and taking part. It was at once an affirmation of trust in the adequacy of the Scriptural doctrine of the Gospel, the church, and ministry as well as a confession of faith in the face of the opposition of the administration of the Synod. Fellow pastors from surrounding congregations were present and participating, much to our joy and encouragement. But particularly impressive to us was the readiness of faculty colleagues from nearby Concordia Teachers College to join in. These men would be called to account for their presence as participants in the Service, and that is what happened in later weeks. There come times, however, when the deepest convictions of the spirit must be expressed publicly regardless of the price that is to be paid. Lutheran Christians, of all people, do well to remember the courage of faith which Martin Luther himself expressed in his declaration before all the powers of church and state at Augsburg in 1517: "Here I stand. I cannot do otherwise. God help me." Reaching such a moment with careful intercession and a consciousness of the unsurpassed worth of confessing the Gospel, one can give thanks for the privilege of such a witness. The blessing is lost if the main motive is foolhardiness or merely defiance for the sake of defiance. It must be positive, as testimony for the chief doctrine of the Christian faith being truly first. Christ's rule in the heart, established by the message of the forgiveness of sins through His redeeming work at the cross and His resurrection, is the one power which holds us to God and to one another. Any other religious doctrine, though it may be true and of God, is not the center. When a human speculation, such as the peculiar concept of the literal inerrancy of the text of the books of the Bible is made to be the center, what results is the off-centering of everything. The entire realm of Christian belief is made to rest on an axis that will not bear it. Everything is thrown out of kilter, and the Gospel itself is wasted. Such conviction is what brings pastors and people together on an Ordination Sunday when the significance of what is being done cannot be taken for granted.

A month after his ordination, Pastor Sorrels had a full opportunity to be introduced to the full range of pastoral ministry at Grace. I journeyed off to England for a week's conference in Birmingham, followed by four more weeks of travel with my family to congregations and clergy on both sides of the Iron Curtain. The time out was right for me. I needed to get away from the immediate matters that had taken up such major energies for the previous six months. It is not a boast but a confession to relate that I cannot manage to get my week well-enough organized to take a day off regularly. I put it down to love for the work and the requirements of ministry to several thousand people, but such a schedule makes it mandatory to back off from everything, get away entirely from phone calls, people demands, and parish routine for awhile.

The week in Birmingham was a stimulating change of pace, spent in the company of people whose churchmanship I have admired and whose writings I have read with benefit for years. Shortly after I entered the ordained ministry in 1954 I read a short book by Leslie Newbiggin, *One Lord, One Church, One World,* and have been influenced by his ecumenical theology and churchmanship since. Newbiggin is the moving spirit behind Selly Oak Theological Colleges which is among the foremost places in the western world today where a lively sense of missionary theology and churchmanship is being practiced. Over one hundred people took part in the weeklong conference on the subject of the congregation in mission in a technological world. David Jenkins and Ian Fraser were other British churchmen who formed the panel of lecturers. It was fascinating to live and study and worship with such a diverse group of Christians—mostly laity—from all over the world for that week. Only forty-five minutes away by car from Birmingham was the Coventry Cathedral, with its celebrated Cross of Nails ministry reaching out to various ministries of reconciliation in troubled parts of the world. I hitched a ride over to Coventry with a young German physician; we had along in his car a Maori clergyman from New Zealand and a public school teacher from Zimbabwe in southwest Africa. Our arrival in Coventry was timed to bring us to the Cathedral in time for a five p.m. Vesper Service, with the choral portion of the Service sung by a boy's choir from some nearby English town. This half hour, coupled with another half hour spent amidst the ruins of the former Cathedral left a lifelong impression upon me. The four of us who came stood in silence before the charred ruins of the old Cathedral high altar. German bombers had turned the building and the city into rubble in a single night on November 14, 1940. After the War, German Christian youth had come across the Channel to spend time volunteering their labor to clean up the burned out shell of the 13th century Cathedral. They left the altar much as it was after the fire raid, with charred timbers set above the altar in the form of a cross. Below the altar there were just two words: ''Father, forgive''. That says it all, and the word of forgiveness from the cross is so unmistakably *the* Good News when it is spoken and heard amidst human conflict and the bitter hatreds which put people so distant from the forgiving Father and from one another. The time, the place, the message all ministered to my soul, and the recollection of it still brings the assurance of victory and hope which the Cross ever proclaims.

The days on the Continent were equally memorable. I met Beverly, our four children, and her father and step-mother in Amsterdam. We had arranged to rent a VW Camper Bus, and Grandfather Joseph took command of a Toyota. Off we drove to the East, stopping for several days at my ancestral roots in the Westphalian town of Luebbecke, then on to West Berlin, East Berlin, Leipzig, Wittenburg, Gotha,

Eisenach, and Dresden. Along the way I found numerous opportunities to meet with parish pastors, hear them describe their pastoral ministries in such varied circumstances as East and West provide. The more I listened, the less inclined I was to regard our problems back at Grace Church, River Forest, as global in scope! One young pastor in Leipzig related how useless the traditional forms of church life were in his pioneering ministry among factory workers where he served. His conversation about his work centered on the quality of ministering among the several dozen families who met with him for worship and teaching in a public meeting hall. Another evening's discussion that gave me perspective on my own pastoral scene back home was with a pastor in his 70's, serving a district of the East German town of Gotha. His two sons, both in their 20's, sat in on the Saturday night visit in his living room. Both had paid a price for their decision to be confirmed as youth. It meant frustration in their efforts to enter colleges and trade schools to prepare for work as adults. But their low-key description of the way of Faith in West Germany was not what they wanted to discuss at length. They wanted to know how we fare in America, amidst such incredible material wealth, social tensions, runaway crime, etc. Yes, they also wanted to know the latest about the Missouri Synod problems! I was astounded that they were as well informed as they were, and I had to work at it to keep the conversation coming back to the subject of their ministry in their surroundings.

A similar evening was spent with a young pastor in a tiny village at the northeastern tip of Czechoslovakia. Karlova still has a hundred inhabitants, the size of the town when my father-in-law was born there 80 years before. His relatives were the soul of warmhearted Slovak hospitality, and the pastor put more than hospitality on the line when he received me and our family in his parsonage for an evening of talk. We conversed in German, but not until he had closed the windows in his parsonage study and drawn the curtains. With a shrug he explained that my presence there in his home would be reported the next day by people who made it a point to observe everything and everyone coming in and out of the church and parsonage. He would go himself to the police station before his informants the following day, telling those in charge that a quite harmless American pastor and his wife and children were over for a visit. He was much discouraged about his work, and the twin problems of traditional neglect of the congregation by adult males plus the pressure applied by the Communist Party on youth who were instructed and confirmed, and all who made regular worship a part of their routine of life. My wife's cousin, a man my age, told us of the consequences of his having communed several years before on the day of his daughter's confirmation. Word of this had traveled fast back to the diesel company leaders. As a skilled engineer, he found that others passed him by on the ladder of company advancement. Here, too, participation in the worship of God brought backlash, and I could not help but think of my ordained colleagues back in River Forest who experienced similar bypassing because they put their convictions into practice in participating in an ordination Service. But the result here was the same as the result there; attempting to muffle a living faith always serves to strengthen it. In Bratislava, a beautiful Czechoslovakian city on the Danube just a few kilometers from the border to Austria, we spent a day with a cousin who is a kind of modern-day Deborah. She is an attorney, working in a branch of government responsible for the care of youth from broken homes. Her husband and she have a tiny flat in a drab row of large apartment complexes, but once inside the place was alive with the marvel of Slovak hospitality, humor, courage, and cooking finesse. She told us of what it means to work on, month after month and year after year, under a totally impossible boss who has played the Communist Party game for all its worth to get where he is. In spite of the fact that he knows nothing of child care and cares nothing to learn of it, she has found a way to work around this epitome of the Peter Principle and makes her energies count for the well-being of youngsters who need foster homes. With laughter, tears, and marvelous, passionate words and gestures, she told us how she keeps her soul nourished. She cannot risk attending public service. The last time she was in a worshiping congregation was in the mid-1960's, when Martin Luther King, Jr., preached in Bratislava. She recounted the text, theme, and parts of the sermon—the miraculous draught of fish and Jesus' word to Peter to "put the nets down deeper". Then she told us, with her eyes dancing, how she and her husband handle their own spiritual needs. He has no key governmental job, so he goes to Sunday Service regularly. Inside his Sunday suitcoat pocket he tucks a tiny tape recorder, "made in our glorious Socialist State, of course" she assured us with a whoop of laughter. He records the hymns, prayers, and preaching, and upon returning she makes technology serve her spiritual needs by getting as close to the worshiping community as the tape cassette can put her.

Such moments with such people put a perspective on things for me. The trip abroad, especially that part of it spent in Eastern Europe, was a powerful reminder to me that God is able to bring His people through narrow straits, and always to make us mindful that the Gospel is the one true treasure of the church. The trip for me was much more than getting away. It was getting with people and ministries which made me aware of how much greater obstacles other Christians face in other parts of the world today. Their word to me was consistent, however. "How does it go with Christians in the land of plenty?" I came back to Grace Church with a clearer perception of where the real challenge lay—not in contention with brothers in Missouri Synod, but in living the Gospel in such a way as to bring a forceful witness to comfortable pagans in our River Forest neighborhood. This was not a new revelation to me. But it was underscored emphatically and helpfully. Inner-church squabbles can be the Devil's slickest ploy to draw Christians off from the main task of our mission, which is those who stand outside the Kingdom and its life-giving Gospel. Church contention can swiftly become all-consuming, the subject of virtually every conversation and the over-arching atmosphere of one's waking hours. It can drain out the joy and verve of faithful living, and deliver us headlong into one of the deadliest of the deadly sins—that which our medieval fathers called "tristia" or melancholy: sadness in the face of the Divine good.

Aaron Sorrels' partnership with us on the staff and in the congregation quickly formed a solid bond. We spent more hours than we should attempting to convine the Synodical Commission on Constitutional Matters of the impropriety of requiring Seminex candidates to undergo colloquy. He, and we with him, smarted under the occasion when he would be icily addressed as Mister Sorrels. Lutherans love to call parish ministers "pastors"; it is a term of affection and respect. But I think those affronts were more of a problem for me than for him. He stayed fully immersed in the daily work of ministering to people, and showed his special gifts for one-to-one ministry with members who needed that quality of evangelical care.

In the September following this eventful summer described, I took some time to outline for the Church Council members what I regarded to be unavoidable issues coming up for the congregation as we continued our life together under the Gospel, Scriptures, and Lutheran confessional heritage. The outline I put together for the September Council meeting indicated that we had three choices, to stay in the Synod in a rather "business as usual" mood, stay in the Synod but under a formal protest against the administration's actions, or leave the Synod. There was not sufficient time in the regular Council meeting to discuss these issues adequately, and so the 18 members dutifully agreed to meet for a special evening—after each one had read and reflected upon the materials I had prepared. That evening came and it went, but I found that I was the only one who seemed concerned enough about these alternatives to wrestle directly with them. The consensus among these good men and women of the parish, each one elected to leadership by the members of Grace Church, was "we'll think about these things for awhile, and do not much more than that at the present, at least". My reaction to their response was an unspoken impatience and bewilderment. But they taught me something of essential importance in ministering to a congregation through times such as these.

It is the lesson of timing. It would have been dead wrong for me to have pressed this agenda, and required continuing priority for it in the light of the principal tasks given us and any gathering of Christians. I went home and remarked to my wife about how I felt, and she helped me get the picture that their wisdom is worth heeding. Weren't they teaching me the basic lesson of the journey to Christians in East Europe? One cannot force the timetable of parish events and congregational readiness to take a major step in the face of a problem. Above all, the pastor cannot manage attitudes and manufacture awareness. Waiting is essential, but not empty waiting. The time is given us to be filled with proclaiming by word and deed the goodness of God. If, in the course of that proclaiming, the obstacles become increasingly stubborn, the people will know that those obstacles must be faced and dealt with. But not before.

Chapter 6

Partners in Faith

One of the many things I found myself noticing with new appreciation as the months and years of our congregation's struggle to maintain its evangelical spirit and ministry is the support of fellow clergy. This was evident to me each time I met with colleagues of the Academy of Parish Clergy, a national network of ministers, priests, and rabbis who were actively engaged in helping each other grow in the art and skills of parish practice as well as endeavoring to lift the standards of the ministerial profession at large. I have been associated with the Academy since its beginnings in Houston in the spring of 1968. Granger Westberg, the godfather of so many innovative ideas in American religious life, had secured a grant from the Eli Lilly Endowment in Indianapolis to bring together fifteen pastors and other churchmen in Houston on Easter Monday and Tuesday of that year.

Easter Monday and Tuesday usually find parish pastors a bit fatigued from the rigorous Lenten Season, Holy Week, and Easter Day schedules, but several days in Houston appealed to me and I was glad for the opportunity to go down to Texas and see what the idea was all about. Our first day of meeting at the Institute of Religion of the Texas Medical Center was packed tight with Westberg's presentation, Reuel Howe following, and very lively discussion of the timeliness of the Academy idea. At 5:30 p.m. Granger produced—right out of thin air it seemed—a most hospitable Baptist layman who owned an automobile agency in the city. He announced that all of us were to be his guests for a steak dinner and an evening at the Astrodome where the Houston Astros were playing the New York Mets. We enjoyed the steak, of course, and settled down to watch what turned out to be the longest night game in the history of baseball. For 22½ innings nobody scored. Finally, in the last of the twenty second inning—somewhere around 2:30 a.m. in the morning—the Mets second baseman let a grounder skip by him so that the Astros baserunner could score and we could all go home and sleep very fast till 7 a.m. We did that (none of us wanting to leave the marathon ball game until we saw the ending!); got to our morning session in the Religion Center, decided without much further discussion to start an Academy of Parish Clergy, went back to the hotel to pick up our bags, and got on the plane for home and some sleep and rest!

The collegiality of the APC was a very strong feature of the movement from the first, and during the 1970's, when pastoral gatherings and church conventions of the Missouri Synod were such increasingly painful experiences, the fraternal spirit and support of the Academy grew in its significance. Particularly in sessions of the Board I felt the warmth of concern for Grace Church and myself. We met three times a year, and I was always reluctant to make any conversation about our situation. But without fail the men and women of the Academy Board would ask me how things were going, what was happening to me personally, and what prospects of peace might be in sight. This was more of a blessing than I could have realized back at the Astros—Mets marathon in 1968! From every quarter of the nation and from all segments of Christian and Jewish clergy, I received personal and written expressions of thoughtful, spiritual, and prayerful support. It was not as though the Academy colleagues always agreed with me, or sought to press for information beyond the boundary of propriety. But they cared and continue to care for me and for us all at Grace. Hearing that care voiced in prayers spoken aloud during the meetings touched me in a profound way and has helped to support the congregation and myself on our journey.

Another circle of clergy support is the dozen ministers and priests of our own communities of River Forest and Oak Park who meet every Friday morning at 7:30 for breakfast, worship, and then an hour of study of the Old Testament, Epistle, and Gospel lessons all of us are following each Sunday. This circle of clergy colleagues has been no small boon in my own spiritual morale and ongoing support. I have always had the feeling that the less others outside our congregation and denomination are burdened by our problems the better, since each pastor and each congregation has its own share of troubles. The initiative the colleagues consistently show in inquiring about us and asking how they can be of any help is a powerful witness to me of how wide and deep the Biblical injunction goes—"bear one another's burdens and so fulfill the law of Christ". Meeting with such fine men, year around at each Friday intervals, helps us get to know each other and our congregations unusually well. This spiritual give and take crosses denominational barriers. Indeed, as we study the texts together and each take a turn in helping unfold the meaning for parishioners in today's congregations, an outsider could never tell who was Methodist, Roman Catholic, Lutheran, United Church of Christ, Presbyterian, etc. This experience, which goes on now into its fourth year and has no sign of stopping, is the richest taste of ecumenism ever given me. It is putting into practical expression the grand truth expressed by St. Paul in Ephesians 4—"speaking the truth in love . . . let us grow up into Him who is the head, into Christ, from whom the whole body is knit together in love".

Still closer in was the circle of support offered by staff colleagues at Grace. On Thursday mornings at 8 a.m., Victor Waldschmidt, Paul Bouman, Gerald Koenig, Lyle Mortensen, Tom Kracht, and Aaron Sorrels and I would meet for an hour before our respective duties of the day began. These faculty members of Grace Lutheran School helped me keep a sense of the parish pulse as the days passed. Our time was regularly devoted to things other than the Synodical controversy, since our primary responsibilities were to serve the congregation and school as called teachers and pastors. That context was the healthiest possible for us to occasionally wrestle with issues related to the Synod. It gave each an opportunity to speak and listen to the other. Without ever consciously declaring this policy, our experience together on Thursday mornings helped us to reach consensus as staff leaders on problems of major importance. Because we have that regular time for conferring each week, we can enter the Church Council meetings and the Voter's Assemblies with a unanimity of spirit. No doubt the parishioners sensed this as we progressed further along the way toward decision-making, and the unity among the staff helped give members confidence that their leadership knew what it was doing.

Not all of us on the parish staff approached the Synodical problem from the same starting point, nor did we all arrive at the same conclusion. Other staff members who took a different stance were free to do so and to act upon their convictions as each saw fit. In plenary staff meetings we occasionally turned to sensitive issues of the relationship of the congregation to the Synod, and the atmosphere remained open for each to speak his mind. But I sensed a reluctance to overload the staff agenda with such matters, and no doubt there was wisdom shown by staff colleagues in not pressing the discussion too loud or long on points of controversy. But for that very reason, the plenary staff sessions never could be as instructive and supportive as the Thursday morning sessions with a smaller number of colleagues—where the touchy matters were addressed and strides toward consensus were being worked out. Reflecting upon that, it occurs to me that people who work closely each day at the serious and joyful task of teaching and proclaiming the faith to children and adults need to keep that task uppermost. When the center of gravity stays on the principal reason why we are called together in service, the door can be opened to also work at hard, delicate problems. They need not be avoided. They need not be all-consuming, either!

But the closest and dearest circle of support was that formed by my wife, Beverly and our four children, Ann and Christopher, Sarah and Joel. Martin Marty, recalling special moments of family friendship in the Foreword to this book, aptly describes my wife's realism and forbearance with our congregation's struggles. So often she had a listening ear for me when I needed to pour it all out, and if I have been known to keep a steady hand on the Grace Church wheel of leadership, it is in no small part due to her love and support, her tenderness and good humor. She has ministered and continues to minister to me. So much of my counseling work brings me into contact with people mired in unhappy marriages. I have long since learned to see more clearly the gift of my own happy marriage and the good cheer which the children also bring to our lives and to me personally. During the days of heaviest pressure through the mid-1970's, our family has been able to get away from time to time to a small island in Lake Michigan where we have worked together to finish the interior of our house there. Banging away on dri-wall installation or lugging heavy beach stones up for our fireplace construction has been the healthiest kind of outlet for us all. It was better than hammering at people or each other!

The Book of Psalms has an earthy, thoroughly Hebraic picture of what it means to belong to people in that unity that is God-given:

> "Behold! How good and pleasant it is when brothers dwell in unity!
> It is like the precious oil upon the head, running down upon the beard . . . running down on the collar of his robes!"
> Psalm 133:1-2

The image evoked may not be the soul of tidiness, but tidiness is not the measure of holiness. Any pastor who has the immense blessing of partners in service who are close in spirit has a power in his life which must never be underestimated. Just to be able to try out thoughts and ideas which are still tentative is of such value. When I have carried ideas in my head but never put them out before another in spoken form, I do not yet really own those ideas. Nor are those ideas fully grown until they meet the test of critique from others. Then of course, it is possible to measure them against the response of people one can trust. It becomes clearer whether ideas are sound or flimsy, whether they deserve keeping or putting aside. The force of the Psalmist's picture of oil running down the head and shoulders and onto the garments of spiritual kinsmen is not first and foremost a rational, critical exercise inside the head. It is an act of life in its wholeness, the spontaneous act of a full bodied sharing of faith and hope and love from motives centered in God's mercy. The closest analogy, I suppose, in our time is the locker room scene after the deciding game of a World Series. When the last out is made, and the victorious team comes together from the field where they have had to work together to win it all, out comes the champagne—poured with delicious abandon over teamates' heads by players who needed each other to get to the goal.

I do not know what it means to be a part of a church staff where acrimony, jealousy, and the petty distancing from one another takes place day in and day out. But my heart goes out to men and women who must carry out their vocation, somehow, in such dispirited setting. That is not only crippling personally, but more seriously, it is a denial of what the Gospel itself brings into being. The Lord Christ creates partnership among His servants, and that unity of soul is itself an important witness to the truth of the message that we preach and teach. Parishioners catch on quickly if those who serve them are together or divided. It is inconceivable to me that I could have come through these past half dozen years in my life at odds with the men and women with whom I work each day at Grace Church and Grace School. Fellow pastors, teachers, secretaries, janitors—all belong together in a community of mutual faith, good will, trust, and the capacity to respect each other when differences of opinion exist. The pressures of our experience have brought us closer together than ever before. Again, we can "count it all joy" when we are put through various trials, for the very testing itself brings to the surface the steadfastness of that unity which is in Jesus Christ our Lord.

The later months of 1976 were taken up with certain seasonal activities with which every parish pastor is familiar. From mid-October on till the end of the year our responsibilities for the financial stewardship of Grace Church's ministry shifts into high gear. My admiration grows for other congregations of comparable size which find ways and means to motivate Christians to keep their offerings coming in at month-by-month intervals throughout the year. For better or worse, our experience has always been that one third of the total budget is received in the final two months of the calendar year.

Reaching a budget goal of $375,000 for a congregation of some 850 giving units is a respectable goal, requiring the best from each member. Month by month our members are given a financial report in Voter's Meetings, and it frequently occurred to me that the most strident critics of our parish direction were those who were virtually silent when it came to giving. The actual information on the amounts given by individual members is confidential, known only to the Stewardship Committee leadership, the financial officers and myself. As Voter's Meeting harangues were delivered by the few whose voice and sentiments were quickly recognized by the membership at large, these financial and stewardship leadership people had to exercise considerable restraint. The temptation was strong to stand up in the assembly and simply state that talk is cheap when support is nil.

It became an increasing offense to me personally, and a reminder of the duty of ministry to admonish people in their spiritual responsibility of supporting the work of Christ's Kingdom, as the disparity grew between talking and doing. People could and did take advantage of every aspect of service offered by our congregation and our day school, but our policy has been and must ever be never to publicly criticize people for poor stewardship. In private conversations with a few members, however, I became more and more aware of the build-up of resentment—if not downright malice—that was finding expression through financial boycott of Grace Church. This puzzled me all the more because each member was entitled to designate his gifts, and a good share of our financial support still was earmarked for the support of the Lutheran Church—Missouri Synod. Any member disenchanted with our growing opposition to Synodical policies could still channel his gifts exclusively for the Synod through our congregation. But that was not the choice of most who opposed us. Instead it was to withdraw all contributions or all but a meager token of the full capacity for giving.

In each December Voter's Assembly our annual budget is presented to the membership for adoption for the coming year. At the same meeting, officers are elected for the forthcoming terms of service. Both actions brought gratifying results. In spite of pressures upon us, our members showed the courage to adopt an ambitious, challenging budget for 1977 and elected a slate of men and women to office who represented a wide variety of gifts, experience, and spiritual maturity.

It was aggravating in the extreme, however, to learn that a

minority group within the congregation felt called upon to circularize hundreds of the homes of Grace members in December, 1976, with a letter that was entirely negative in tone and content. With the final push on to meet our commitments, this expression was so contrary to the spirit of the Advent/Christmas season. I must say that more than any other letter that went out unauthorized, this one from a handful of members convinced me that a core of people within the congregation were not going to relent in their determination to undo everything the congregation stood for in the interests of turning us around to full support of the present administration of the Missouri Synod.

But when the temptation would come down hard on me to get angry and sullen about these things, the experience of preaching never failed to bring me back on course. That Sunday-by-Sunday discipline of putting myself under the Christ of the Holy Scriptures, and proclaiming His truth to His people at Grace, showed me the invincible power of the Gospel and the *healthy* consequences of preaching when the pressures are on. The whole experience of Sunday worship was oasis-like for us; without worship we could not have made it. Never did worship and preaching appear more central and essential.

The year ended with a record outpouring of offerings which brought us the good news that the congregation met its commitments. It would seem that such news would be welcome to any and all who know even the slightest about congregations as voluntary organizations working very hard to keep the spiritual motivation for support centered on the Gospel and the response in giving an appropriate response of faith in the risen and living Lord. But as we passed from the old year into the eventful year, 1977, I recalled some lines of Hilaire Belloc, that as we strive to do our faithful best, we are watched by those who stand apart, and on those faces there is no smile.

In the closing weeks of 1976, another disturbing development came from Hong Kong concerning one of the most distinguished theological educators in the Missouri Synod. Dr. Thomas Coates was summarily refused continued support from the Synodical Board of Missions in his teaching ministry at Concordia Seminary, Hong Kong. No reason was cited, but Coates' staunch advocacy of inter-Lutheran cooperation in the overseas ministry of the Gospel was enough to put him at odds with the Preus administration. Here was a man in his late sixties, still in excellent health and at his maximum capacities as an educator of young Chinese for the ministry in Hong Kong. He had been president of Concordia College, Portland, Oregon, and later a much respected faculty member at Concordia Senior College in Fort Wayne, Indiana. For decades he had made a major contribution to the worship life of clergy and laity within and beyond the Missouri Synod through his attention to the spiritual life of the Christian. Coates is anything but a contentious individual. Yet he did not hesitate to speak his mind in the face of what was happening to Missouri Synod Lutherans overseas as well as in the United States. Hong Kong had been the scene of one of the more bizarre efforts on the part of extremist Missouri Lutherans to portray their more evangelical brothers as guilty of moral as well as doctrinal lapses.

Thomas Coates had been a good friend of Grace Church and of our former pastor, Otto Geiseman. It was natural, therefore, that Grace congregation members approved putting a full support figure for Dr. Coates in our 1977 budget. That support has continued through 1978 and is scheduled to extend through 1979, providing a personal link between Christians in River Forest, Illinois, and Hong Kong.

Another related development had occurred in the summer of 1975, when the ultra-conservative bloc of Synodical clergy and laity passed a measure at the Anaheim, California, convention which in one stroke dismantled a whole system of pre-seminary education which had been carefully constructed over the previous twenty years. The Senior College at Ft. Wayne, Indiana, was put out of existence by a majority vote of delegates. The public relations rationale for the measure was to remove Concordia Seminary, Springfield, Illinois, from that location to Ft. Wayne to occupy the Eero Saarinen-designed buildings of the Senior College campus. The Senior College faculty was comprised of many of the most gifted younger theological minds in the Missouri Synod, and it was sending students to the seminaries who were not viewed favorably by the Synodical administration. The Springfield Concordia Seminary faculty, however, was presided over by Jacob Preus's brother, Robert Preus, who saw to it that the faculty and curriculum was thoroughly acceptable to the administration plan of revamping seminary education throughout the schools of the Synod. This meant that several dozen Senior College faculty were out of their jobs within a year.

The consequences of all this for individuals on the Senior College faculty had been brought home forcefully to our member, Walter Christopher, who had come to know Dr. James Childs through mutual service on a committee appointed by President Jacob Preus to attempt to bring some plan of reconciliation out of the chaos of the Synodical scene in the mid-1970's. Nothing came of the committee's extensive work except the publication of a thoroughly documented report which was laid to rest on many church office shelves in congregations of the Synod. Mr. Christopher sat through numerous hours of meetings in St. Louis with James Child and had come to admire this gifted young theologian whose acumen was needed in the field of his specialty, Christian ethics.

In the late spring of 1976 Grace Church had established a theologian-in-residence program. This addition to our ministry was made possible by the memorial fund donated by Mrs. Bernice Feicht in memory of her late husband, Arthur. The purpose was to bring into our congregation for a portion of each year some person with particular gifts, who could both enrich the spiritual level of the parishioners and be enriched by the experience of being in a congregation for a time. Childs had been given a two year contract in 1976 to teach theology at Valparaiso University in Valparaiso, Indiana, which put him within an hour's commuting distance of River Forest.

In the fall of 1976 he became a most useful "displaced person" at Grace. The hardship of being put out of a job at the Senior College led to new opportunities which would not have occurred if tranquility had prevailed in the Missouri Synod. Childs was put to work with several dozen carefully selected men and women of the congregation and given the assignment of spending some hours with each one at the place of work where these members spent the majority of their weekday time. The span of jobs these laity held was varied, and as the months went by, Childs got to know people in their workday settings. His purpose in spending time with laity at their work locations was to learn from them and with them what connections exist between faith and work, worship on Sunday and job on Monday, the world of the congregation and the world of work. This venture continued throughout the fall of 1976 and the winter and spring of 1977, and was a valuable experience for us all. His hours spent with Robert Lamont helped him see the surprising satisfactions as well as obvious burdens of a committed Christian who teaches history in an all black high school on Chicago's west side. His time with Hans Biebrich helped him see the challenge and difficult ethical decisions this member faces in keeping the work going among the largely Puerto Rican work force in the wholesale meat business on Chicago's Fulton Street. Thelma McManus gave him insight into how it goes in handling the candy department at downtown Marshall Fields store during the week, and traveling every weekend the forty mile distance north to the Veteran's Hospital to visit her husband, a permanently disabled World War II veteran. William Tatman, an Illinois Bell vice president opened up to him some of the aspects of his duties in keeping tabs on all the motorized equipment of that giant business, but—more important—in dealing with great numbers of people who work under him. Caroline Kallas, a psychiatric nurse, shared with Childs her exceptionally sensitive religious insight into her work with troubled people, as well as some of her own feelings concerning the bringing up of her youngest child who suffers from Downes Syndrome disease. From Emil Gotsch he learned what the Word and sacrament and the supportive fellowship of the congregation mean to a man who has had two companies close their doors under him in his working career. And so the list continues, through twenty-four people who were interested in the fact that the congregation was this interested in them. A more detailed description of the issues and impressions these lay Christians reported back to the congregation is contained at the end of this book (See Appendix B, pp. 173-77).

These insights gleaned from Dr. Child's sessions with lay persons at their places of work say much about where Grace members are in their major concerns and interests as Christians. The general themes running through could be related to virtually any group of serious congregation members in the religious groups of America today. What is striking, of course, is the sharp difference between these daily concerns of life on the job and the agenda of items delivered to parishioners month after month in the religious controversy with the denomination. This variance makes it all the more remarkable that lay people can find the energies required to think through and act upon a whole set of problems not directly related to the things primarily on their minds between Sundays. No pastor, and particularly no pastor of Grace Church, should take it for granted that lay people can get interested and stay committed to the demands of working through the problems of the congregation. The more I think of this, the more inclined I am to say that if the matters brought before the laity do not have any ultimate connection with their struggles in the arena of the workday life and vocation of Christians, they do not deserve a place on the agenda.

In the light of these conclusions, what is more evident than the truth that God's people living out their faith in today's world need support and edification in the congregation, not futile bickering and pointless wrangling over matters that were not genuine doctrinal deliberation at all. As we turned the corner into 1977 the issues seemed more and more clear. In order to keep our parish energies centered on things which truly relate to faith active in love in today's world, we had to face the question of how and where they can best be done as a congregation. In the early fall of 1976 I had learned that the Church Council, at least, was not ready to wrestle with that question. Six months later, however, things had changed sufficiently to make that question unavoidable. Members had experienced six more Voter's Assemblies that were burdened with the drone of accusation and disruption. The parish had seen one more gifted overseas missionary summarily terminated from Synodical support. The negative letters circulating the parish and the growing discrepancy between what James Childs was telling us and what the synodical controversy was requiring of us helped to bring about a change of attitude among a growing number of Grace members. Only a very sick person in spiritual matters would want to keep going in endless contention. At the end of the January, 1977 Voter's Assembly I made a passing remark in my general pastoral report to the members that, in my judgment, the time was coming to "fish or cut bait". At the close of the meeting I was astounded to find that people from all points on the spectrum came up to second those sentiments heartily.

Chapter 7

Exercising Accountability

The winter season in 1977 brought record cold and snow to the nation, giving people everywhere a new appreciation for every oasis of warmth and every harbinger of spring on such a wintry landscape. At Grace Church, like everywhere else, we winced at fuel bills and kept shoveling back the snow and ice as Epiphany gave way to Ash Wednesday and the Lenten Season.

The time seemed right for a breath of springtime freshness after the long winter of our Synodical discontent. And so, with the elders and the Church Council, I worked on a statement of goals for the congregation that could rally us in our deepest convictions and fondest hopes as a people under the Gospel of Christ. The work was not unilateral on my part. It was truly a joint effort, with particular help coming from George Reinhardt and Edward Erickson of the elders group, and Don Koetke of the Youth Council of the congregation. I should explain that the Church Council of Grace congregation is comprised of three elders, three trustees, three youth council members, three financial officers, the treasurer, with various staff members of pastors and teachers sitting in as advisory members. The Council meets each month in joint session, one week before the Voter's Assembly. Frequent extra sessions were scheduled by the Council to complete a carefully worked out expression of the genuine spirit and style of Grace Church, past and present. We did not realize it during these demanding sessions together, but the experience was preparing us to work, think and speak together to the congregation later on in the year when more exacting communications to the congregation were required of us.

We did not make the following statement something for the members of Grace to vote on. Many of us had already had more than enough experience with expressions of a spiritual nature that were voted on in Synodical Conventions and then declared "binding" on the entire denomination because they were declared to be a flawless expression of the very mind of God in the Scriptures. Voting on the most sensitive issues of the soul, with the purpose of then requiring everyone else in the community to assent if the margin is at least 51% of the vote, is an affront to the Holy Spirit. Christians can and should vote on many matters that have to do with the practical decisions of property, business procedures, etc. But voting on belief is the Devil's tactic.

We therefore presented the following statement of Grace Church goals as a way of stating quite openly and honestly the convictions of the elected and called leadership of the congregation. Our sense is doing this was that the people have both the right and the need to know what our mind was as we looked toward the future. The things which counted above all, the spiritual vision which we prized as paramount for the ongoing ministry of the congregation was the thing we wanted to offer our brothers and sisters. And we asked for their help in shaping these imperfect expressions more nearly to the Biblical pattern for our life and service together. Here they are:

GRACE CHURCH GOALS

At this time in the life of our congregation, we seek to express our faithfulness to Christ our Lord and address certain issues before us. We do so by expressing our assent to these goals:

1) We remember our tradition as a congregation and do not repudiate it.

We have many blessings to count during the past 75 years of

our relationship to LCMS. At certain times, however, the members of Grace Church have expressed dissent from Synodical directions. Former Pastor O. A. Geiseman's participation with 44 other Missouri Synod clergy in protesting the legalism and isolationism of the Synod in 1945, and his vigorous protest of the Synodical action of 1959 in making a Brief Statement binding carried with it the support of the congregation. In this time of unprecedented Synodical turmoil, we recall the tradition of faithful members and clergy before us in Grace Church, who kept the Savior's love and the sole authority of the Scriptures over the decisions of humans which threaten the freedom that is ours in the Gospel. We intend to continue this tradition, looking to God for the grace to believe that He will supply all things needed for His church.

2) We desire to be soundly Lutheran in our profession of faith and not fall into sectarianism.

We define ourselves doctrinally as a Lutheran congregation by that standard which unites all Lutheran Christians: the Holy Scriptures of the Old and New Testaments as the written Word of God and the only rule and norm of faith and of practice, and the three ecumenical creeds (the Apostles' Creed, the Nicene Creed, the Athanasian Creed) and the Symbolical Books of the Evangelical Lutheran Church as a true statement and exposition of the Word of God. We reject as un-Lutheran and un-Biblical the recent actions of LCMS conventions which have made doctrine and Biblical interpretation binding by majority vote of conventions. We regard these directions as sectarian, not Lutheran. We will not substitute power politics for Lutheran churchmanship because that has proven divisive and ruinous to too many ministries of faithful brothers and sisters in the Synod in recent years. We define ourselves according to Article II of our congregation and the Synodical constitution, and seek to continue a way of evangelical congregational life that flows from that essential spiritual source.

3) We intend to keep fellowship with other Lutherans and not cut ourselves off from them and other Christians.

Our pulpit and alter fellowship with ALC Christians, expressed especially in the Word and sacrement shared with members of nearby United Lutheran Church in Oak Park, is a gift we rejoice in and thank God for. We seek the expansion of such pulpit and alter fellowship, and oppose the announced intentions of the LCMS administration to call that fellowship into question. Furthermore, in the conduct of our pastoral ministry here at Grace we welcome clergy of other Christian traditions to add their words of Christian prayer and Scriptural encouragement to couples of mixed denominational affiliation in weddings in our congregation, and we are glad for our pastors to do the same when invited. We oppose restrictions which prevent us from learning from other Christians as well as sharing our spiritual treasure with them in our congregation and school. We do so because the Scriptures teach us to do so. We stand in unity with all Christians as we profess our faith and respond in joyful faith to His Word. We cannot help or admonish each other by isolation. Our loyalty as Lutheran Christians is to Christ and His Church, as we say each time we speak the Creed. The institutional commitments and loyalties we take responsibility for are motivated from and judged by our primary loyalty to Christ our Savior Himself.

4) We recognize the priority of God's mission to people in our communities around us and the world beyond our neighborhood, and will not obstruct that sacred task by continued embroilment in Synodical controversy.

God calls us into existence as a congregation for the sake of those who do not yet hear in faith the gracious Word of His Son. In our words and deeds of witness, through our congregation and our school, His mission is being carried out. But that primary purpose of our existence has been increasingly obstructed in more recent times as faithful members of Grace Church have been formally accused of false doctrine, and harassed in their ministries by accusation of Synodical disloyalty. Our members have been misled and confused by a steady barrage of unauthorized publications from outside and circulation of unauthorized letters from within our congregation. These distractions take our time and energies from our mission. Furthermore, we cannot expect that new converts will find the peace and joy of Christ in our midst while these attacks upon us continue. We will not continue to invest our time and resources in futile Synodical disputes, and we confess our full reliance upon God's Spirit to show us the right path into the future, and our partnership with other Christians in mission.

5) We desire to strengthen our spiritual life and fellowship within the congregation and not wear ourselves out with Synodical strife.

The harmony we enjoy at Grace Church is an undeserved gift of the Holy Spirit. We confess our sins against the unity He creates. We recognize the problem of increasing strain on that harmony in the past several years. But we shall not be intimidated or fearful in the face of problems. Instead we wish to be more helpful to each other in resisting the acids of secularism which erode our lives in family, work, and public duty as citizens. The demands of ministering effectively to one another into divisiveness is sin. Every member of Grace Church is called to join together at the source of our unity as a congregation: the preached Word and Holy Communion. We dare not neglect that source, but use the means of grace to keep us together and help us grow in our stewardship of talents and money, the expansion of our ministry of education through our congregation and school, the enrichment of our fellowship and service through every activity of our congregation. We need each other as brothers and sisters in Jesus Christ, and by His grace we will not be divided into warring camps. Powerful forces are at work to destroy the tender bonds of faith and love which miraculously hold us together, but our trust is in God Who is greater than these forces and Who does all things well.

We commit ourselves to these goals in the hope of God's favor and blessing in Christ, Who is the church's one foundation, our joy and our strength for time and eternity.

At the meeting of the congregation in which these were presented there was spirited discussion in support of the document, a member rose to make his motion that it be adopted as a definitive statement of the congregation vis-a-vis the issues which had been troubling us for some years. But the assembly wisely laid that suggestion aside, and accepted the proposal of senior elder, George Reinhardt, that they be thought about, prayed over, and further elaborated by any who wished to offer their helpful counsel. There would be no time in which these sentences would be formally adopted. They had served their purpose in communicating the sense of direction on our part as leaders and inviting everyone to reflect more deliberately upon their content and their implications for all of us.

They also served to elicit a strident reaction among some of our members, whose numbers may have been small but whose determination to oppose these directions of leadership was not small. We would be learning more about that opposition in later months of the year.

But such things should not come as an unwelcome surprise to congregational leadership. Every evangelical thrust will be met by a counter-thrust of an opposite spirit. Count on that. It will never be different as long as we are on this side of heaven. It is a strange truth, often overlooked (and a lamentable oversight it is!), but the forces which run counter to the primacy of the Gospel in the church were never so stirred as when people confess openly and freely an unqualified trust in the sufficiency of the Gospel as the one and only foundation on which the congregation stands. Our Lord Himself laid down those terms to His church in His last great discourse to the disciples before He went to His cross. He spoke of those who would seek to destroy the Christ-given spirit in people and regard that effort at annihilation as service to God. He spoke of travail, of sorrow, of tears as the people of Christ strive to carry His message of the New Age into the world. All of that He promised as the inevitable experience of His people. We need to hear that, since our temptation is to think that once we have said the Good News or put it into a carefully worded document, the opposition will roll over and play dead as the triumphalist church marches to "victory". It is not that way. The embodiment of the Gospel in a world and a worldly church which seeks security elsewhere, and resents the scandal of the cross brings sharp reaction. His word to the church is, however, to keep the vision of faith centered on Him and to rejoice because He has overcome the world. That's what keeps us from morbidity and in discipleship. A "theology of the cross" in Luther's words keeps in perspective our frustrations, anxieties, and failures. When the counter thrust against the Gospel spirit is what is vexing us, then—of all times—comes the time for a quiet remembering and rejoicing that these things which seem to never go away are the expectable signs of following Him Who promised us exactly what we are experiencing. The point is not to dwell on how difficult our experience is, but how sufficient for all these things the Crucified One is. The result of that is deepening of faith, strengthening of character, and the sustaining of hope.

The sense of preparing for an approaching decision began to take more tangible form in the later weeks of Lent. A consensus was reached at the leadership level in the Church Council that if the members of Grace were to be asked to make a decision on Synodical affiliation it was necessary to give people an adequate basis to come to that decision for the right reasons and at the right time. The proposal was made by the senior elder to the Voter's Assembly in mid-March that three informational meetings be scheduled to discuss practical and spiritual matters that had to be aired before responsible decision-making. The Voter's Assembly approved the schedule, which called for a March 29 meeting on matters related to our property, staff pensions, Grace School, and our relation to agencies of mission and benevolence which were not owned and operated by the Missouri Synod. Next, a meeting was set for April 20 in which the president of the Synodical district in which Grace participates would be asked to speak as well as myself on spiritual concerns. Finally, a May 2 meeting was scheduled to follow up on any matters carried over from the previous two sessions, as well as a look to the future.

These three meetings were then announced to the entire membership well in advance. It was explained that no decision-making was to take place in these sessions. Their purpose was to provide information, answer questions, raise new issues heretofore unrecognized, and hear all sides of the issues. It was also announced that the Church Council proposed that the Voter's Meeting on May 17 be the time when a Council recommendation on our relationship to the Synod be decided.

The meetings were exceptionally well attended, with upwards of three hundred parishioners present for each. Printed materials on the practical concerns of withdrawing or staying in the Synod were provided the members attending the first session. It was a learning experience for many, who heretofore never really thought about the bread-and-butter issues of pensions and medical insurance which had always been supplied through excellent plans of the Synod itself. At that March 29 meeting, reference was made to a letter from the secretary of the Synod in St. Louis, and copies of it were provided for all who wanted to read it in detail. He conveyed to the members a strong appeal to stay in the Synod, with the additional reference to the opinion of the Synodical attorney that if we withdrew from the Synod we would surely be faced with the Synod's decision to repurchase our property and church building. The opening and closing sentences of that letter were pious exhortations for us to stay in the denomination. But the bulk of the letter was a statement in no uncertain terms that they would seek to take our place of worship and our school facilities away from us if we did withdraw. That letter said much more than the words and sentences themselves. It came across to most of us as a threat, an unworthy and ungraceful way to speak to a congregation that had been struggling to keep its support of the Synod intact in spite of the profoundly troubling actions the Synod had exerted on respected Christians within and beyond Grace Church. What we missed altogether was *any* desire on the part of the Synodical officials to hear us out, to learn of our circumstances, to put themselves in our shoes, to see what was happening to our evangelical directions as the controversy wore on. What we got was a threat. If that was the intention of those who conferred on that communication to Grace Church, I wondered if they had any idea of the effect it had? For several years we had been hearing of forced removals, power politics, and thinly veiled threats given to recognized, experienced men and women in teaching posts, administrative offices, and mission ministers. Here was Exhibit A of that alienating spirit addressed to Grace Church itself.

But in the face of such a threat, the meeting was calm, rational, and deliberate. The overall message was that Grace Church and Grace School could function outside of the Synod as well as within it. Nothing more, nothing less.

The second meeting, nearly a month later, came on the second Wednesday in Eastertide. The packed assembly hall heard President Edmund Happel of the district office of the Synod deliver an altogether sincere appeal for Grace congregation to remain in the Synod. No agenda was set for him, other than an outline of the scope of all three meetings. He was free to say to us whatever he chose to say, and his choice was to stress the value of staying with the denomination institution in spite of whatever we felt was lacking within it. That approach was cogent in its own way, since every one of us could rightfully withdraw from a difficult situation simply because we found it inconvenient. But what was needed from our president was emphasis on the main issue of our ministry under the Word to the community at large and the strengthening of our mutual ties as Christians within and beyond the Synod. That we did not hear, although the discussion following President Happel's presentation was often steered that way by questions from the floor.

My own turn came that evening to speak from my heart to the congregation. What I said came as no surprise to anyone. But it was the first time that I took thirty minutes to attempt to lay out as clearly as I could the decisive spiritual issues before us. What counts above all is the confessing of Christ, and all genuine doctrinal give-and-take among Christians must be toward the upbuilding of brothers and sisters rather than winning points over opponents. Since we were in the Easter season, it seemed appropriate to take the Gospel for the previous Sunday, the disciples walking with their risen but unrecognized Lord to Emmaus, and address the particular doctrinal issues in that Easter light. There are two doctrines involved, I said. One was the doctrine of Holy Scripture, the other the doctrine of the church. The problem as I saw it was that the Synodical leadership had introduced new, alien criteria to the question of fidelity to the Bible as the inspired Word of God. Inerrancy was now the touchstone of orthodoxy, the particular kind of inerrancy which called for exactness in interpreting statistics, geographic references, and chronological details which the Bible does not ask of itself. All of us in the denomination confess our faith in the Holy Scripture as God's own work and gift, and the only source and norm for our faith and life. But we have that conviction because the Bible proclaims God's mercy for the world in Christ Jesus His Son. We do not have that faith because of a man-made theory of inerrancy. The Emmaus conversation of our Lord with the disciples makes the simple, essential point so clearly: "O foolish men, and slow of heart to believe. . . . And beginning with Moses and all the prophets, he interpreted to them in all the scriptures the things concerning himself." The Christ-centered doctrine of the Scriptures is the Biblical teaching concerning itself. The Missouri Synod was in a state of chaos because that center was being removed to a philosophical concept of inerrancy not clearly grounded in Scripture.

The other issue concerns the church, the gathering of Christ's imperfect, forgiven people. His Spirit-given life in the congregation always leads us together. Unity is not optional, it is the gift and mandate of His cross and resurrection. The power in the church that avails and upbuilds us all in love is the power of the Gospel, and there is other power by which the church can be the church. The sad story of purging faithful ministers, abusing power in bringing accusation, judgment, and expulsion against faithful brothers and sisters, the increasingly sectarian spirit of withdrawal from all who do not conform to the Missouri Synod standards of orthodoxy, the offense of yellow journalism sowing seeds of distrust and disruption among the people of Christ—is not the Church of Christ. My appeal to the members was to understand ourselves as the flock of Christ rather than a branch office of a denomination institution, and to chart our course by the Bible rather than the primacy of by-laws from the denominational handbook which were being used to override the Biblical teachings of the church.

The third meeting on May 2 was again a full house, giving me a deep sense of pride and gratitude in the interest shown by that many parishioners in what was going on. After review of previous meetings and additional discussion, one of our senior members and probably as respected a person as we have in Grace Church arose to ask that we delay action until September.

Wilfred Kruse, emeritus professor of Concordia College

and veteran of so many Synodical conventions and congregational meetings, was heard and heeded. There were sound reasons for postponing decisions until the fall. We were asked to secure our own legal opinion on our property status if we withdrew from the denomination. We were asked to await the outcome of the July convention of the Missouri Synod convention in Dallas, Texas.

Waiting was no problem for me. If the decision to stay or withdraw could be reached only because of haste, it would surely boomerang. Some of our members were disappointed with the thought of delay. But they gave assurance that they could live with such a mild dose of impatience. Their greater concern, I perceived, was that the Synodical leadership and its counterparts within Grace Church had four more months to generate mischief in our midst. My own view was that those efforts served precisely the opposite purpose, and I felt confident that waiting was not only prudent but the faithful thing to do.

Late in June the three elders and I went to St. Louis for a day to meet with the committee of the Board of Directors on the question of what the Synod would do if we withdrew. Their answer, given in the context of a fraternal atmosphere was that they did not know. They had been able to secure an opinion from their lawyer that our withdrawal would trigger Synodical action to repurchase our property. But they explained to us that the remaining months of 1977 following the Synodical convention would find the Board of Directors swamped with a demanding agenda of administering a church program among some 6000 congregations affecting nearly three million people. The question of when the Board of Directors would come to some decision on what to do about Grace Church, River Forest, in the event of our withdrawal would in all likelihood not find a place on their agenda until early in the coming year, 1978.

That point registered in my mind, and I confess that a question mark hovered over it all the way back to Chicago that evening on the plane. I learned that the same question was in the minds of our elders, George Reinhardt, Edward Erickson, and William Tatman! Within three months we would have our answer, for the Missouri Synod took exactly ten days to act against us following our September 20, 1977 decision to withdraw!

I do not want to imply that the Missouri Synod Board members who met with us that June morning in St. Louis were playing games with us. I can only assume that the three were telling the truth when they said they did not know whether the lawyer's opinion on our property was also the Board's opinion. They were no doubt right in saying they did not know whether the Synod would honor our step to independent status and still recognize our ministry as valid in the full Lutheran sense. They were, after all, only three men representing the Board and could not speak with finality on what the leadership of the Synod would do if Grace Church withdrew from denominational membership. The one thing they could say with certainty to us was that the Board's answer to our dilemma was to stay in the Synod. After giving us the courtesy of listening to our delineation of our parish situation, their response was unchanged and the only thing we could properly conclude from the conversation that day was that they were sincere.

But less than three months later we had a clear answer to the questions we were asking as to the intentions of the Missouri Synod toward Grace Church. We voted to withdraw from the Synod on September 20, 1977. Precisely ten days later, on October 1, 1977, they told us of their decision to repurchase our property.

The second step we were asked to take had to do with the securing of a legal opinion on the contract Grace Church had signed with the Synod in 1929 to purchase the two acres of land on which the sanctuary and school were built. Where to go for that?

During my several years vicarage in Japan, from 1951-

1953, I had come to know Otto H. Theiss, an able churchman and theological educator in the Missouri Synod who had also been a close friend of the former pastor of Grace Church, Otto Geiseman. During the years following the friendship with Dr. Theiss in Japan, I had come to know his son, William Theiss, an attorney with the prominent Chicago law firm of Kirkland and Ellis. Our own member who was an attorney, Mr. Walter Christopher, agreed with the suggestion that we take our problem to Theiss and the Kirkland and Ellis firm, which we did. Thus began a renewal of my contact with William Theiss and a larger opportunity to observe his professional skills in action. In this day when the legal profession comes under criticism—often enough deserved—for being riddled with lawyers who are mainly interested in exhorbitant fees to use language no one understands for the purposes many find questionable, it is more than refreshing to find attorneys who take seriously the Dominical injunction to be wise as serpents and innocent as doves. Theiss is of that quality and working with him opened my eyes to the workings of the legal profession and court system in a new way to me.

The particular issue facing us was the proper legal meaning to the terms of the land contract between Grace and the Synod signed in 1929. That agreement provided, among other things, that the Missouri Synod may exercise an option to purchase the land and improvements of Grace Church in the following circumstances:

—Whenever Grace Church decides to "affiliate, consolidate or merge with any other corporation, association not affiliated with the Missouri Synod, or

—Whenever Grace Church shall "fail or decide not to teach and preach the scriptures as set forth under Article II of the Missouri Synod constitution and in accordance with the rules, regulations and customs of the Missouri Synod.

The background for that agreement begins in 1928, when the congregation was located in Oak Park, Illinois, a half mile from our present site in River Forest. Having outgrown its church facilities then, the congregation approached the Missouri Synod with the proposal to purchase two acres of the land on the square block of Concordia Teachers College. The Synod responded by refusing to sell the land, instead proposing a lease arrangement. This the congregation would not accept. Next the proposal was an agreement which insured that the church would remain with the members loyal to the Missouri Synod in the event of a falling out between the congregation and Synod. This, also, the people and pastor of Grace Church rejected. What finally resulted was the wording quoted above which produced a contract that some regard as unenforceable.

It was Mr. Theiss's and the Kirkland and Ellis law firm opinion that if Grace Church should choose to become an independent Lutheran congregation, still holding to the same doctrinal confession of faith as that of the Missouri Synod, the Synod's claim to be able to buy our building from us is without merit. This judgment was well grounded and it became an important component in the thinking of the congregation leaders during the summer of 1977.

The third assignment given us was to await the outcome of the mid-summer Synodical convention. The convention came and went, with no sign of returning to its former even-handed style of letting no single party dominate, stressing the Bible over by-laws, the maintaining an evangelical spirit in its internal relationships. In fact the ultra-conservative group which had steadily grown in power over the previous half dozen years succeeded in putting the declaration of pulpit and altar fellowship with congregations of the American Lutheran Church under a cloud of doubt and suspicion. The formal term for this was entering into a status of confessional protest against these fellow Lutherans who did not measure up to the new Missouri Synod standards of doctrinal correctness. Those not familiar with these inter-Lutheran problems are properly mystified by the spectacle of Lutheran disunity. All three major Lutheran bodies in the United States have the identical standards of faith, the Holy Scriptures, the three great Creeds of the earliest centuries of Christendom, and the body of doctrinal confession which came out of the 16th century reforming work of Martin Luther and those who shared his passion to restore the church to its Christ-centered tradition. The news, then, from Dallas was not heartening to us. And to many, the increasingly sectarian direction of the Missouri Synod at its 1977 convention came as no surprise. The manner in which those in power reached their posts was well enough known, and few who knew that story expected them to change their outlook.

The time had come for the Church Council members to meet squarely the question of remaining in or withdrawing from the Missouri Synod. This meant nineteen men and women working very hard to keep the particular question of denominational affiliation under the larger, more central issue of keeping our congregation centered in the Gospel and in continuity with the evangelical spirit of its years of service and mission since 1902. In the later summer weeks, our Council members met faithfully to chart a course that began with the conviction that Grace Church should withdraw from the Missouri Synod to continue its ministry and its mission as an independent Lutheran congregation, still identified by its traditional confession of faith (which is identical to the Synodical confession of faith). That conviction, accompanied by a question and answer document explaining the reason for this recommendation, was mailed to our members in early September. At the heart of it was this expression of hope for our present dilemma and our future course:

> "(We hope) . . . to put behind us the crippling Synodical controversy and the serious spiritual disruption that has invaded our Voter's Assemblies, pastoral ministry, and worship life in the past half-dozen years. We confess our own sins in the breakdown of love and trust among us. We re-state our support of the confessional basis set forth in Article II of our constitution . . . As an independent Lutheran congregation, still based on the fundamental articles of faith which unite us with all Lutherans and which form the bridge of unity with all Christians, we wish to focus our energies, our gifts, our resources on strengthening each other for the great task of living the Gospel in an increasingly secular world and sharing God's grace with all who are without it . . .

The resolution to withdraw from the Synod had the unanimous support of the entire Council, and each member signed his or her name to the document which was then mailed to each family of Grace Church.

Among those members who opposed this proposal was a Concordia faculty member, George Nielsen. He had been meeting with the planning group of Grace parishioners who asked the Church Council to circulate their letter of opposition to all the families of the congregation prior to the September 20 meeting. The Council agreed to do this, but would not agree to send a letter of March, 1928, written by Dr. O. A. Geiseman at his initial contact with the Synod for the purchase of the property. Knowing Dr. Geiseman's sentiments at the time and throughout his 40 years of ministry at Grace Church, none of us could condone the measure which would seek to twist his letter into a document of support for those advocating continuing membership in the Synod. Nielsen agreed with this conclusion, but came back a day later crestfallen because the group was adamant in its insistence that the Geiseman letter had to go out with the minority letter. Instead of sending their own appeal letter, without the Geiseman letter, the group chose to send both letters in their own mailing to congregation members. It struck me as an irony that those who complained so vociferously that Grace Church refused to abide by the procedures of the Synod did not abide by the efforts of their own congregation to give them a full and fair hearing prior to the time of decision.

The first half of September brought days and evenings that were extra full. And that was a welcome blessing to me personally. The sick and troubled needed Word and sacrament. Couples were in for the purpose of preparing for marriage. Our school resumed its fall schedule, with the customary flurry of activity brought about by 290 children again in our halls and classrooms. Several deaths in the membership occurred in that time, and when ministering to people in the time of bereavement everything gets pulled back into proper perspective. Another welcome event in the well-filled schedule was participation in a Conference on Wholistic Health another brain-child of Granger Westberg's fertile mind and imagination. The meeting brought to Chicago people of national leadership in the fields of medical education, health insurance, and hospital administration. I was invited as a member of the Academy of Parish Clergy, and found the sessions thoroughly stimulating. Every hour that was thus occupied was appreciated, because the nagging layer of concern that was underneath everything else that occupied me during those weeks was the outcome of our congregation's decision.

And then came the 20th day of September, the decision meeting for the congregation, and the decisive vote to withdraw from the Synod which has been described in detail. The sun rose as usual on the morning of the 21st. The universe stayed in orbit, the world continued on its way. In our small corner of it, however, a step had been taken in order to bear witness to a very much larger conviction about how Christians can live and work in the freedom of the

Gospel in today's world. That step had been taken with the best kind of preparation we knew how to give it. The people had been prepared, and all the resources for decision making that we could supply were offered.

September 20th was a good day for Grace congregation. I could not have been more proud of the courage and conviction our members displayed.

With that decisive step taken, we looked ahead, wondering and awaiting whatever was in store for us.

CHAPTER 8

The Same Grace Under New Pressures

We were not kept long in waiting for the Synodical administration reaction.

Our vote to withdraw was known to people in various parts of the country before midnight on the evening it was taken. This might sound strange, or even presumptuous. But for better or worse, Grace congregation is one of a number of congregations which receive attention beyond our immediate membership. The Chicago papers gave it prominent coverage, and our action was an item on the religious news service national wire services.

On October 1, ten days following our decision, the Missouri Synod Board of Directors sent us word of its determination to purchase our property and buildings for $750,000. The document was handed to me by President Paul Zimmerman of Concordia Teachers College, who had asked me to come to his office to meet with him on the afternoon of October 3. The meeting was brief, as its chief purpose was for him to hand-deliver the Board of Directors' decision to me and to Grace Church. I read it over in his office, noted the ridiculous offer of $750,000, and asked him how that amount was determined. He said he did not know. Without further comment I excused myself and walked back to my office.

The walk back afforded me a fine view of the buildings of the congregation and school. I thought of the sacrifice the faithful people of Grace Church during the decades of the 1930's and 1940's when the struggle was so exhausting just to meet the payments on the interest of the building mortgage! A host of stories came back to my mind about the individual commitments of little-known men and women of the congregation who gave themselves with sterling dedication to the surmounting of that immense debt during the worst years of economic depression in our nation's history. A host of people, not known to us anymore, but dear to God, put their heart and soul into the support of the ministry of the Gospel—and Grace Church as a building is a token of that faith. Above all, I thought of Otto Geiseman, who kept the level of leadership so consistently Gospel-centered as everyone wondered where the next payments would come from. God alone knows how many personal visits, personal letters, personal phone calls he made to rally the congregation to meet its commitments month after month, year after year. And by 1948 the building was debt-free! In 1952 another major wing was added to the facilities of Grace School, increasing its capacities to serve boys and girls from throughout our area—non-Lutheran as well as children of families of the congregation. And that new wing was paid for by 1956.

Throughout the years of that monumental labor to pay off the building debt, Grace Church continued to keep up its regular commitments to the Missouri Synod. Year after year, when voices were raised in complaint of carrying a crushing building debt *and* supporting the wider work of the Missouri Synod, the decision was always not to curtail the latter while laboring at the former. After the building debt was paid off, the congregation remained among the leaders in contributing to the support of the Synod. In 1967, when the Synod had sent out an appeal for congregations to contribute to a Thankoffering, the Grace Church response of $88,000 was at the top of the giving of all the parishes. Such a history is not boasting in ourselves, but in the power of the love of God in Christ to open our hearts and stir in us the spirit of giving. Those experiences were no burden to the people of Grace Church, but great blessing, and they are recalled as a thanksgiving for the grace given us at Grace Church.

The document I had in my hand, now, however, contained an altogether different spirit. It was as though the leaders now making decisions in the Synod had turned their backs on relationships which had been built over long years. Now, the primary thing was that we were not members of the organization. But what we believed, prayed, taught, and practiced as Lutheran Christians under Christ Jesus our Lord did not seem to count. In the judgment of the Board of Directors of the Missouri Synod, we were no longer fellow pilgrims working together under our one Lord, but adversaries who had property that had to be returned to denominational control.

That decision of the Missouri Synod Board should not have surprised us. A half year *before* we took the action to withdraw from the synod, their legal counsel had advised them of his opinion that if Grace Church should withdraw from the denomination for independent status, the Synod should take action against us to purchase our property and building. Nothing had occurred to change that opinion of their lawyer following our June, 1977, visit to the Board of Directors. Yet, it remained a lawyer's opinion and was not yet a Board action. Their decision on October 1, however, made it clear to us that the lawyer's opinion had now become their Board's decision.

What very few of us understood on October 1, 1977, and what many interested persons still could not realize, was that the action of the Missouri Synod Board set in motion a legal process. The original contract stated that if the option to purchase the contract is activated, both parties have thirty days to agree upon the price. If a price cannot be agreed upon in thirty days, an arbitration process is to follow during the next sixty days.

The Board claimed, without substantiation of any kind, that they had the right to repurchase our property. They named the price of $750,000 (for property and a church and school building which—conservatively estimated—is worth millions of dollars). In their minds, the proper legal process was in motion. They expected us to inform them of our decision as to the price within thirty days, and if there was no agreement on $750,000 to enter into further negotiation in the following sixty days.

If we would have simply informed the Missouri Synod Board that they did not have the right to repurchase the property and improvements, and that all discussion of the price was out of order because the *right to buy* was not theirs, they would have had us in court after ninety days for failure to comply with their interpretation of the contract. This assumption on my part was confirmed by our legal counsel, who knew far more about land contracts and the law governing their implementation than I did. The Missouri Synod Board had published a statement urging the avoidance of litigation in questions involving church properties, but their statement clearly indicated their acceptance of the necessity to do so under some circumstances. We, too, had stated our seriousness about the I Corinthians 6:1-8 admonition of Paul to the Christians of Corinth to steer clear of heathen courts as a place of settlement for disputes among Christians. The October 1 decision of the Synod Board put that question squarely before us.

The first thing to be done was to ask our legal counsel to confer with the Synodical attorney for the purpose of finding some fair way to settle our differences over the land contract outside of court. A group of Missouri Synod leaders met with our elders and me in Chicago later in October to talk together about possible solutions. The principal suggestion of theirs to us which I recalled out of that meeting was that the Grace Church membership contact the nearest American Lutheran Church congregation to us and inquire if we might not move out of our church and merge with them! That session only clarified for me the impossibility of dealing with the basic question, the right to buy Grace Church. They felt that was settled, and the only question was the price. Not long after that meeting, the Board proposed to us a three-man panel of jurists, all to be Missouri Synod members, that we would all agree upon as the court of decision—with no right of appeal. We could not accept the proposal of three Missouri Synod members settling the dispute in which the Missouri Synod itself was one of the parties.

While these unsuccessful attempts at finding a proper means of settlement were proceeding, the Missouri Synod representatives were meeting with a group of Grace Church members who opposed our withdrawal from the Synod, an act which did not increase our confidence that the Synod was desirous of dealing with the congregation in full seriousness in finding an out-of-court solution to the question. Our decision was to inform the Synod that we remained open to discuss with them the fundamental issue of the differing interpretation of the land contract. When we received no positive response from them on this question, and thirty days was soon up, the congregation took the question to the Cook County Circuit Court and filed for what is called a declaratory judgment of the court. Specifically, our plea was that the court declare our right to continue in our church and school; and that our action of becoming independent did not invoke the terms of the land contract. This was not a decision easily reached. The congregation had given the Church Council the authority to act in its behalf in these delicate and difficult questions. After several lengthy and very intense meetings of the Church Council, the conclusion was reached that under these circumstances it is not sinful to seek a proper legal defense of our rights to continue in the place which our members had built and paid for years earlier. It was a legal contract under dispute. The Missouri Synod had no religious court to handle questions of real estate law. For us to have attempted to establish an ad hoc court on the basis of three Missouri Synod members who might be available did not appear to us as a responsible solution. Our decision to take the matter to court was based on the conclusion that the Missouri Synod is not and should not try to erect an entire legal system which parallels the courts of the land. Even as we make use of hospitals and regard them as channels of God's providence, so we chose to use the legal institutions of the land as a means of achieving justice.

Having said all this, however, the decision to take our cause to the court came only after reluctance, struggle, prayer, and the awareness of our own imperfections as a group of believers at Grace Church. It was one more instance in which one does the best he can under the circumstances, and still prays for the forgiveness of sins. Only the devel would gain if we would look back over this incredibly difficult and complex struggle with a sense of smugness, thinking that we were entirely right and our adversaries were entirely wrong. When Christians are called upon to decide something in areas that are gray instead of black and white, the deciding has to be done. But the forgiveness of sins is always needed for our best efforts which are also imperfect efforts.

No one in the congregation was delighted to be in court. All of us, including each member of the Church Council who participated in the unanimous vote to take the matter to court, took the step with a heavy heart. As the congregation members affirmed that step in the November Voter's Assembly by a resounding majority, it was still with a sadness over its necessity. None of us possessed a crystal ball with the answer to when the court would decide and what that decision would be. We sensed that we had turned in a new direction and that the path would be lengthy, trying, and not a little expensive. On the matter of covering the legal cost, the congregation resolved that all legal fees would be paid out of a special fund created for that purpose; nothing would be taken from our regular offerings. The cost of litigation was ours to bear, but it could not prevent us from meeting our regular commitments as a congregation.

A remarkable thing has occurred in response to this additional challenge. People have shown such generous capacities for giving—far beyond anything we could have assumed or imagined! College students away at campuses have sent in their contributions. A friend of our congregation, who had been remembered in the will of an aged relative in Norway she had cared for, came in one morning in the spring of 1978 with an extraordinarily generous check for our legal defense fund. Another member arranged for an entire restaurant to be reserved for a benefit dinner in the mid-summer of 1978. The 300 person capacity was filled to the limit, as Grace members and friends enjoyed one of the happiest and most zestful evenings we could remember. And $8000 was added to the support of our cause that evening. Two Chicago symphony trumpeters arranged with our music director and organist, Mr. Paul Bouman, to present a benefit concert in the spring of 1979 in behalf of the Grace Church cause. The all-important thing remains the widespread, steady support of the membership as a whole. In 1978 our members contributed a total of $35,000 to this special fund. Meanwhile, the members met and exceeded our regular commitments in the congregation and the mission agencies we support beyond Grace Church. In fact, total giving in the congregation increased by approximately 20% during 1978, the first full year we were out of the Missouri Synod and at the same time shouldering these additional costs.

Financial stewardship is only one index of a congregation's spiritual health, however. I realize that I am not the most objective commentator on the congregation, but I am not alone in sensing a growing vibrancy in worship and deeper appreciation of one another as fellow members in a congregation that was indeed experiencing grace under pressure. People came to us seeking affiliation because they knew what we were about and what we had been through. Fellow members of our staff have experienced a closeness in spirit as never before. People showed an increasing willingness to serve in the varied offices and service organizations of the congregation. Membership and worship attendance have not dropped, but inched ahead. We have found that the responsibility of planning and carrying out our wider network of partnership and support with ministries of the Word at home and overseas was more carefully thought through. Members who have the skill and experience in retirement and medical insurance helped us fashion new and adequate programs for our staff of 18 people. From beyond our membership there have been numerous words and gestures of support and encouragement. We might have taken these for granted before, but not now. Everything we do takes on a sharper edge of meaning and purpose during the months following the fall of 1977. The mystery of "counting it all joy when meeting various trials" is being unfolded to us. The testing of faith does produce steadfastness, "with its full effect" (James 1:2-4). We are but one small link in the long chain of generations of Christians who have learned these things. Looking at it all in this light, we have far more to be thankful about than to grumble over.

Pressures have tightened upon us from those who have taken issue with our direction as a congregation. The Synod felt it necessary to have its commissions on adjudication take action against us—a year after our withdrawal. Another suit has been filed against the congregation by six people who alleged that the congregation has been misled all along. The administration of Concordia Teachers College informed us in the spring of 1978 that we would henceforth have to increase our playground insurance five-fold and pay a sizeable fee for the use of playground space on adjoining college property. Our Grace School children have played in this area for over 45 years without a formal lease being signed. But all these things did not really surprise us. They are symptoms of a mindset and a way of church life which places human traditions and power over the Christ-given spirit of love and mutual upbuilding in relationships. That is why we withdrew from the Missouri Synod for independent status, so that we could continue to carry out our life as Lutheran Christians under the Holy Scriptures and the Spirit of Christ without being trapped in the alien spirit which has come to dominate in the administration of the Synod. The fact that we encountered reaction and additional difficulty should come as no surprise, nor are we entitled to complain about it. As long as all this serves to make us more mindful of Christ Jesus as the Shepherd and Guardian of His congregation and the whole church, something good is redeemed out of the whole experience.

But it takes stamina. And sad things do happen. This came home to me sharply in the experience of meeting with numbers of member families who felt it necessary to transfer their membership from Grace Church to congregations still affiliated with the Missouri Synod. These splendid parishioners were the families of members who drew their paychecks from the Synod as professors at Concordia Teachers College nearby us. It was not easy for them to come to this decision, and the pain of parting was felt by them and by others of the congregation who miss their presence. While I did not agree with their decision of transferring, I could only respect their sense of integrity in doing what they thought best under the circumstances. Some other families sought membership elsewhere because of a loyalty to the Synod. But withdrawing from Grace Church was not something done lightly, for some deeper ties were uprooted in these relocations of membership. Some members have decided to remain on the membership roster, but have taken up their worship and fellowship elsewhere. This is explained as an act of protest, but it is an offense to Grace members. No constructive purpose is served thereby. In fact people do themselves and others a positive harm by giving their absence from Word and sacrament in the congregation a covering of righteousness. Some family members suffer silently as they are required to go along with this in order to keep marital and family peace. Those silent sufferers deserve pity rather than scorn, for their hearts are still at Grace Church but to assert that conviction will only throw their personal lives into greater distress. And not every Grace Church member has agreed with our majority decision. People are busy with other concerns in life, and do not bother to examine thoroughly the questions involved. It strikes them as unnecessary that their congregation has to go through all the rigors of the past several years. After all, the thinking goes, life in the world has enough problems. The congregation ought to be a haven from conflict, not an addition to it. How this point of view handles all the New Testament statements about Christians having to face conflict *because* of our faith is not thought of seriously. But such members need patience and understanding no less than any others. Who could assume that 1750 people all move at the same level and pace in spiritual understanding and maturity? It does not happen that way on this side of eternity.

What do members themselves have to say who have been a vital part of the life and work of Grace Church for many years? It is well for several of them to speak their minds in these pages and I have asked several to do so. Anyone who knows anything about Grace Church will know and respect Mr. Fred Schmitt, a layman who has held office within the congregation and been active in worship and fellowship in the congregation for more than fifty years. Here are his words:

"The fact that I began my membership at Grace Lutheran

Church in 1914 puts me in the camp of those members of the congregation who can be called "old-timers" I suppose. I do not think that sheer longevity of membership makes us qualified to rule over other parishioners, for God's Spirit sends His wisdom on young men and maidens as well as His older servants. (Joel 2:28-32.)

"But I begin with a testimony of being a Grace Church member for over sixty years because I am humbly grateful for it. I have had the opportunity of living through hard times and wonderful years in the congregation. It is been given to me by the Lord to see the congregation pass through changes—without losing our center in the Gospel of Christ. Along with other older members of Grace Church, I can recall our struggles in planning and building our place of worship and our school, and am ready to give praise to God Who saw us through those days of the Depression when we didn't know from month to month how we were going to meet the mortgage payments—let alone wipe out the capital debt. But it happened! And we were the better for having faced those challenges in faith that the Lord is able to do far more than we ask or think.

"My lifetime association with Grace Church includes a period of time serving as an officer of the congregation and thus sitting in on the Church Council planning. I recall especially well the time in the 1940's when Grace Church backed our pastor (Dr. O. A. Geiseman) fully in his desire to keep us going in an evangelical direction. He got a great deal of opposition from some Missouri Synod leaders and pastors. But that was because of a strong evangelical spirit coming into contact with so many of our man-made ideas about what we could and could not do as a congregation. We all had a lot of growing up in Christ that we needed to experience, and looking back over those years I am all the more grateful for the courage given us in the Gospel.

"In more recent years, I saw with my eyes and felt in my

heart the struggle of keeping on the same track our congregation followed in earlier decades. When the Missouri Synod leadership changed in the late 1960's so abruptly, it finally meant a hard decision for our congregation as to remaining within it or stepping outside it. When the time came for the vote, I felt we had no other choice. We had to move away from a denominational controversy that was tearing us apart and diverting us from our real purpose—witnessing to the Savior's love to our community and world instead of engaging in controversy that kept me and many others awake for too many sleepless nights. In the earlier stages of this entire problem I thought we would surely stay within the Synod, since many of us have known the Synod and loved it all our lives. It has been my privilege to also hold office in our District, and the hours of service I have put in as the former treasurer of the District I will never regret. For they were hours spent in service to Christ and His people. But, as month after month and year after year went by in the early 1970's, I gradually came to see that we had no other choice. Along with a strong majority of our members, including our long-standing members, I supported the decision to withdraw from the Synod.

"I do not know what the final outcome of the court decision regarding our property and building will be. Naturally, I hope it will favor our continuing in this place of worship which has meant "home" for us over the years. Furthermore, I hope that future generations of people—young and old alike—will continue to find Christ preached here and His Word honored here, as we have done and still do. But the building is not the Kingdom of God. The Gospel in the hearts of people, giving us all the grace to worship God sincerely and love people faithfully—that is the real church. And that church will never disappear.

"Therefore I leave it all to God's wisdom. He has led us faithfully this far. He will not fail to bring His will to pass in the future. If we but keep Him first, we are going to see again and again how much He can do!"

Another parishioner, Mrs. Ruth Zeddies, reflects upon the more recent decisions of the congregation in the light of her membership at Grace which covers nearly twenty-five years:

> "In reflecting upon my twenty-four year association with Grace Lutheran Church words come to mind like—gentle, kind, caring, sharing, giving, loving—all attributes of a Gospel-oriented community and a natural response to membership in the Body of Christ. When I recount the blessings in the lives of my family, foremost among them is our Grace Church experience. Sunday after Sunday we come to join happy, positive, Christ-loving people to hear a spiritually profound exposition of the Word of the Lord, and to be uplifted further by the organ, the instruments, the choirs, all giving praise to the glory of God's name. We are further blessed with Grace School, its excellent Christian education program and dedicated teachers; with the adult Bible classes, the in-depth study of the Word and its social implications which has been taught by well qualified, experienced teachers, and a first rate music program giving my family an opportunity for participation in the choirs.
>
> "Despite this positive note one cannot escape the difficulties with which our church family had to deal in recent years. Decisions by the Lutheran Church—Missouri Synod administration had an adverse effect on the scholarship and the ministries of many called servants of God. Amidst these trying circumstances our congregation came to the aid of our brothers and sisters in upholding their innocence in the face of charges of false doctrine. We opposed the un-Lutheran action of the Synod in declaring that convention votes on doctrine made them binding. That is contrary to everything we know to be Lutheran and is against the Synodical constitution itself. With the ever increasing legalism and political maneuvering of the Synod our ministry and our very existence as a congregation came under attack to the point that our association with

the Synod had to change. We wanted an end to the insulting attacks on our pastor and the senseless bickering by a minority group. We wanted to get on with our ministry to the parish, the community, and world sorely in need of Christ's comforting Gospel.

"We are saddened by the move out of the Synod into independent status, for this has changed our longstanding association with Concordia College which until recent years had been pleasantly reciprocal. It has meant a strain on our relationship with friends who seemingly could not part with an institutional affiliation. It has meant the pain of seeing members who now refuse to share with us the Body and Blood of Christ in Holy Communion.

"However, Grace Church, despite past difficulties, has been lifted above this human condition and remains the congregation it has always been. The Word continues to be source and norm of faith, and the creed we speak in our worship services still expresses our faith in the living God. Our future we surrender to the grace of our Heavenly Father. Whether we are housed in a cathedral-like building or a simple store front, His invitation is our invitation: "Come to me all who are heavy laden and I will give you rest." And His command is our mission, "Go therefore and make disciples of all nations." Although our location is on a thoroughfare named Division Street, we are not divided as members of Christ's body. We shall by His grace continue together with our varied gifts toward the strengthening of our life and our mission under Christ.

"We made a decision on the evening of September 20, 1977, an evening that I shall always remember. But nothing essential and eternal has changed!"

These two members speak for so many more, who truly desire a genuine applying of our deepest convictions as a congregation to our present problems (and blessings) and our future prospects. I am overwhelmed by the privilege of serving such people, and the thought of continuing together into the future makes my heart glad.

We do not know the particulars of the things coming. We cannot pretend that those particulars do not interest us greatly, but they are penultimate. The ultimate certainty we possess, and share with the whole Church throughout time and space, is Who is there to meet us at each turn of the unfolding future. Our Lord Jesus Christ shall be there, even as He is here. Learning better to trust Him now is possible because of that future He holds out to us all. His grace is always under pressure. That is the circumstance in which we best grasp the sheer wonder of His power and goodness! And so, Grace Church has the gift of living under some pressures during these times which we hope can send out rays of light and hope to partners in the faith near and far. Our experience is not the most dramatic test of the faith of this or any other century by far. It is one modest testimony to the sufficiency of Christ's promise to be with His people till the end of the age. But in, with, and under our particular experience lies the power of the Gospel to give people courage to act upon the best of their convictions when the temptation is strong to be unfaithful by doing nothing. And that is what courage is: grace under pressure.

APPENDIX A
Summary of Issues

	English District	*N. Ill. District*
Relation of the Synod to the Congregation:	Synod is advisory; congregation is autonomous and is free to determine what is best for its mission & ministry under Art. II of LCMS Const. T.	Congregational autonomy is there, but congregation must honor & uphold the resolutions and by-laws of LCMS.
Role of District President:	DP is servant to the congregations which call him to his post as their representative.	DP is an officer of the LCMS and an extension of the LCMS's president's authority to the congregations.
Causes of unrest:	Loveless treatment of brothers, centralizing of Synodical authority; unprecedented campaign of slander against faithful brothers, illegal changing of doctrinal basis by making Preus *Statement* binding by majority vote.	Breakdown of Synodical loyalty and thoroughness of traditional LCMS indoctrination; human pride and intellectualism. Formation of power blocs such as ELIM.
Solution to unrest:	Enlightened Bible study at the parish level, instead of cliches about the Word; forthright support of mistreated brothers; maintenance of congregational autonomy in order for congregation to stay with the main thing: mission and mutual ministry under the Gospel.	Care not to destroy congregations by obsession with strife; use District materials to get at issues, honor & uphold Synodical resolutions and to pursue regular channels of dissent.
Vision for future:	Freedom to follow God's Spirit in what new directions He is preparing for people of the LCMS; care for people who have been hurt by strife; continuity with the real treasure of LCMS tradition as expressed in Art. II; withstanding legalism and authoritarianism; keeping the mission of the Gospel and the practice of brotherly love uppermost.	Continuance of the NID as defined in the new polity of the district; maintaining fellowship with those with whom the LCMS has declared fellowship; honoring resolutions and regulations in order to walk together harmoniously; see the challenge of the diverse urban and rural mission of the NID.

Calling a new assistant to our staff:	Recognize the congregation's right to call and ordain a Seminex graduate as well as a St. Louis or Springfield graduate.	Calling a Seminex graduate can mean expulsion from the LCMS, unless he is certified by LCMS.
Grace/CTC relationship:	Not qualified to predict full implications, but probable problem with the CTC administration.	Strained relationship.

APPENDIX B

Summary of Lay Responses to Faith-Work Issues

In preaching and teaching the church needs to be as specific as possible in applying the word to the issues, (even issues like the economy) problems, sins and temptations of daily life. This is not only a help to people in translating faith into daily life but it also reassures them that the church is aware and concerned about what is going on in their day to day world.

Sermons should be such that they challenge our minds and give us solid food to chew on. (This is not to say necessarily that the sermons of grace have not been.) Assurance of grace and forgiveness is important but must be unpacked of its meaning for daily life.

People in our sector of American society need to be made more consciously aware of "middle-class sins". We all tend to become financially overextended and perhaps too deeply involved in business commitments. These entanglements reduce our options in life and tempt us to compromise service, family life, religious life, and moral principles. There is a temptation to take easy outs like having an abortion rather than a baby who would disrupt the delicate balance of the life we built.

There is a need felt by many to nurture and support family life. The pressures on today's family life are tremendous. The vocation of the woman as homemaker needs serious and thoughtful reinforcement, especially in view of the influence of the women's movement. (see section VI Proposals)

Decision-making is a major part of most people's jobs and daily life. Some basic help in Christian decision-making is strongly desired.

There is a basic need for help to the Christian in just coping with the fact that one is daily surrounded by secularity. I think that a first step in that help requires that Christians understand what the secular outlook is, what its problems are and the sort of "faith" it represents. Perhaps then we might also understand the Christian faith better.

There is a genuine yearning for fellowship among many, an opportunity to share problems and insights with one another relative to the kinds of things we focused on in this project. For some in the group the most important thing in the church experience is the fellowship opportunities.

Others stress as important an increase in one to one contact and pastoral visitation. We are understaffed pastorally. I think this kind of meeting that we were having were it to happen with the pastors on a regular basis might be well received in most people's minds.

On the other hand, one person noted that one tends to be a bit reticent with thc clergy: "We can't be ourselves."

People in business often have the problem of "wishing their lives away" by always being geared to the advancement, security and retirement benefits that lie years down the road and therefore, by ignoring the opportunities and joys of the present.

There is agreement among quite a number in the group that we could do more with utilizing the resources possessed by our members in the whole process of Christian education.

One person suggested that we might work more on community at Grace, i.e. know more about one another, our work, our interests, where we live, etc.

Most people think of the relationship of the Christian faith to daily life in terms of morality; i.e. concern for business ethics, concern about how to respond Christianly to those with whom one is in conflict on the job, concern to make morally responsible decisions, concern for being honest and hardworking, concern for being fair with others, etc. Sometimes this concern may take shape in a refusal to take part in certain business practices or even agressive opposition to certain morally dubious company policies.

For some there was an admitted difficulty in connecting faith and life in terms of witness to Christianity. It is hard to witness when job roles prevent you from confronting people with things they need to hear. It is also hard to witness when you feel you don't know how.

Others made the significant observation that Christian witness is something that must be integral to the whole personality. People will not give an effective witness by some how-to technique; it must come naturally from a person whose life is formed by Christ.

Witness happens in terms of how one treats people on the job: with respect, with care and compassion, with fairness.

There is a need for Christians to be more involved in politics and public affairs. More Christians should be in government. Christian presence is very important in shaping society toward the good of all.

Some, who occupy classrooms, have a special opportunity to make their convictions known in connection with their teaching and in even bringing religion in as a subject matter.

Daily Bible reading and prayer before and during work is a helpful way to keep one's Christian faith a part of each day's life.

A Christian perspective on life, knowing one is accepted by God in Christ and thus a person of value with an everlasting future, is an antidote to life in a performance-oriented world in which we are judged by our success or failure. (see section v)

Christians out of their concern for others can make an important contribution to the good of society even when their jobs don't seem to be directly concerned with the public welfare. For example, one doesn't need to be a professional environmentalist to make a contribution to improved ecological conditions.

Some would have to admit that they find it difficult to say

with certainty that their Christian faith operates in their daily life. However, I think this may be as much a problem of lack of experience in answering such a question than it is an indication of the absence of faith's influence in daily life.

Christian people in the contemporary world, especially those who are in a scientifically oriented profession, can feel a real tension between aspects of the anti-supernatural scientific outlook on reality and traditionally understood precepts of the faith concerning God's actions in human affairs.

Christian faith functions in daily life by enabling one to establish a set of values and priorities in life. This observation though true could profit from more specificity.

Closely associated with the previous point is the observation that Christian faith finds expression on the job when the Christian sets an example of representing humane values and self-giving love in a setting that is thoroughly secularized, materialistic, self-centered and amoral.

A different form of Christian witness emerged when certain people shared this project with co-workers in anticipation of my visit. The interest of those co-workers was remarkable and perhaps significant the possibilities for sharing the faith when it is tangibly related to the job.

Some are able to identify the service they do in their work for people and family as an extension of or a channel for their Christian service of love.

Being a Christian and knowing Christ and his salvation infuses life with confidence and hope. This general perspective is a part of daily life as well.

Faith should be strong when things are good and not simply a refuge at times of trouble.

One of the problems of relating what happens in church to one's daily life is that work seems more concrete and immediately meaningful in itself.

Primary relationships in which there is a shared faith

together with church life itself is a help in resisting some of the temptations and allure of the secularized lifestyle that surrounds a person.

Faith is more readily understood as a part of life when we realize that God is at work in and through all things including institutions and individuals that are not necessarily Christian. One realizes, then, the potential value of our daily participation in social, political, professional and economic institutions as occasions and channels of God's activity.

For some, perhaps all, really, the fundamental relationship of the Christian faith to life and daily work is that, despite the ups and downs of job or the business, God will pull me through and take care of me. There is confidence in His love and guidance. Ultimately, He is our only hope!

"A person needs to be fed." This signals one important contribution that the church makes to daily living. We need the strength that comes from regular gathering around Word and Sacrament.